ORKNEY: A PLACE OF SAFETY?

ORKNEY
A PLACE OF SAFETY?

ROBERT BLACK

CANONGATE PRESS

First published in Great Britain
in 1992 by Canongate Press plc
14 Frederick Street Edinburgh

ISBN 0 86241 350 8

British Library Cataloguing in Publication Data

A Catalogue entry for this book is
available on request from the British Library

Typeset by Hewer Text Composition Services
107 Ferry Road, Edinburgh

Printed and bound by Butler and Tanner
Frome, Somerset

Contents

This is the story of a chain of events in Orkney before, during and after February 1991. It is the story of a number of families who were caught up in a situation outwith their control, when nine children were taken from their island homes and flown to mainland Scotland. It is a story of secrecy, lies and evasion. It tells what can happen when many of those expected and trusted to protect children and their rights misuse the powers vested in them and ignore rules, guidelines and lessons of the past.

If the following chapters seem to be weighted in favour of the parents, that is because their decision to fight back was a public one, and they were prepared to talk openly about everything that was happening to them. Those in authority were not, so obviously their input is less, but this book aims to be honest in spite of the complexities.

I have a great respect for the essential work that social workers do, and understand the pressures under which many of them operate. These are not just the sheer volume of work, but also the financial limitations that face them every day, but the best interests of the children are, and must always remain paramount.

I am a member of a Children's Panel in another part of Scotland. I believe that the Children's Hearing System in Scotland is far superior to the English alternative which deals with children within the courts, but any system has to change and develop to accommodate the times in which we live.

During the research for this book it became apparent that not all Hearings are conducted in the same way throughout the country. In some areas it seems the Reporter has too great an input during the Hearing, and in others the Panel is too ready to accept Social Work recommendations without question. It may be that, because of very heavy case loads in some areas, and the essential confidentiality, that the System has developed in different ways. In this book the chapter on the operation of the Hearing System tells the way it should and does run in many areas of Scotland – this does not seem to have been the case in Orkney.

When Lord Kilbrandon put his name to the Report which would lead to the establishment of the system in 1971, I wonder if he imagined just what an impact it would have on the care and protection of children.

This story has been told because of my belief in the Hearing System, not because I want to be sensational, but because the events in Orkney have added to already substantial pressures on the System, and it must be protected from those who want to destroy it.

I had occasion to be in Orkney during the time when the events recounted here took place. Like many others I had my suspicions at the beginning; I wondered what had really been going on in that small island community, and whether a group of incomers were indeed involved in sexually abusing their children. In my work on the Children's Panel I deal with cases where children have been physically, mentally and sexually abused by members of their families and others. I am not blinkered, nor, I hope, am I biased, but in Orkney as the events unfolded and I learned how checks and balances built in to protect children and their families had been disregarded, I realised this book had to be written.

'The Best Interests of The Children' was a phrase that came readily to the lips of everyone involved in the case of the nine South Ronaldsay children, but I question whether what was done in Orkney was ever truly in their best interests.

Robert D. T. Black
September, 1992

CHAPTER ONE

The Dawn Raids

At dawn on 27 February 1991 nine Orkney children were taken from their beds by social workers and police, and flown away from their parents and their island homes to 'Places of Safety' on the Scottish mainland.

At seven o'clock on a dark and dreary February morning without any warning, several cars arrived simultaneously at six homes in South Ronaldsay, the most southerly of the seventy Orkney islands, and also at a caravan home in Kirkwall. Between four and six police officers, together with as many as five social workers, descended on each of the homes. Within minutes they had roused sleeping children from four of those homes and driven off with them into the murky winter dawn. The children were given no explanations, no assurances; only the oldest of the nine, a fifteen-year-old boy, was told they were to be questioned for a day.

Some of them, wakened by the noise, as what seemed like crowds of people poured into their homes, crept downstairs to eavesdrop. Terrified, their initial reaction was to make a run for it; but other considerations crowded in. The fifteen-year-old boy leapt from his bed with escape in mind, but he decided it would be unfair to leave his eleven-year-old brother to face what was to come alone, so he got back into bed and waited for the social workers to come upstairs. A twelve-year-old, who listened at the living-room door to what was going on, wanted to run, but knew he'd be followed. He went back to bed and wept until they came for him. The social workers even followed him into the bathroom. There was no escape.

The nine children, aged between eight and fifteen, were upset and frightened. Yet it seems that none of them was completely surprised. Only four months before, eight South Ronaldsay children, all from one family, had been taken into care from school in front of all the other pupils. From that moment, all the island children believed that social workers could come and lift children from anywhere at any time. All of them lived with a nervous expectation that it could happen to them. The home of those eight children, now occupied

9

only by their mother and a family friend, was another of the six South Ronaldsay homes visited by police cars at 7 o'clock that morning, and the caravan in Kirkwall was the home of the oldest son of the family.

Involved in offering succour and assistance to the mother of those eight children taken from school was the local minister. At that time the Reverend Morris Mackenzie, a New Zealander, and minister of the local parish, had invited Mrs W – as we shall call this mother of fifteen children – to use his manse as a sort of sanctuary. That manse, in sight of the sea, was also raided at seven o'clock on Wednesday 27 February. Police knocking loudly at the door woke the minister and his wife, demanding entry to search. The search was thorough and a number of items were removed; there was talk of ritual sexual abuse.

It emerged that the Reverend Mackenzie, in his sixties and far from well, was alleged to be at the centre of such rituals. A man who may be described as a little eccentric, he suffers from angina, and only a few weeks previously had taken ill with an attack while on holiday in Majorca. In February 1991 he was still far from well.

This was the man alleged to be leading rituals involving island children. There was talk of a quarry, ritualistic music, dance and dress. From the manse the police took away the minister's cloak, a long black cloak with a hood that he used for funerals, Remembrance Day services, and other outdoor events associated with his ministry; they removed a broken cross, waiting in a cupboard for repair; but they did *not* take the broken-off piece of that cross which was lying at the bottom of the same cupboard. They had a warrant to search St Margaret's church and the church hall and removed masks normally used in a nativity play, and Mr Mackenzie's work diary from the previous year with all the religious festivals marked in it. They took other vestments, tapes of services and a camera.

Without a warrant they also searched St Mary's, another church within Mr Mackenzie's parish. He was, he said, too confused to stop them, although he believed the request to search the church was quite improper, and that the police had acted illegally. A number of personal papers were taken away too, together with a hot water bottle bearing the name Benji, and clothes that Mrs Mackenzie had purchased for some of the children in the family of fifteen.

Lastly they took the Minister and his wife, Jan, and drove them fast in separate cars across the Churchill Barriers that block the eastern approaches to Scapa Flow, to Kirkwall, the county town on Orkney's mainland. Both said the police paid scant attention to Mr Mackenzie's ill-health, only allowing him to get a jacket at his wife's insistence.

At the islands' police headquarters they were detained for questioning for four and a half hours. The minister said he felt disorientated, the blinds were drawn, and he lost track of time. The police told him of the allegations from three children, but were, in his words, 'fairly vague' about the questioning. They asked him if there was any truth in the allegations, and he felt they were desperate for evidence. He believed the authorities had decided what had happened, and were looking for things to fit. After the questioning, Mr and Mrs Mackenzie were driven home again to the manse on the edge of the village of St Margaret's Hope.

The pattern was the same at each of the four homes from which the children had been snatched. Some of the parents were taken to Kirkwall Police Station, others to Stromness as Kirkwall was full. The parents of one family weren't taken in for questioning at all that day, but Mrs W was. Two days later, the parents told their story at a public meeting in the village hall in St Margaret's Hope, a little fishing village on the edge of Scapa Flow. At first sight everything seemed normal as boats bobbed at anchor in the little harbour, the wind whipped up the sea, and the mainly farming community attended to early calving.

It was only when no parking places were to be found anywhere near the hall that it became clear that this was not normal. Nothing in the South Ronaldsay community would approach normality for a very long time, and most people from the village and the surrounding community had turned out to discover for themselves what was happening, and then to lend their support to the stricken families.

Already the national press and media were gathering in this tiny island. Hard-bitten journalists hot on the heels of a sensational story had flown or sailed to Orkney by any means they could, as the news broke. Cynical almost to a man, they expected the worst, and had come to write their stories of poor abused children, evil parents, and the things that 'incomers' get up to in remote islands.

As the parents in turn told of their experiences that Wednesday morning, so attitudes changed perceptibly. The descriptions of the dawn raids matched so exactly, and they were given simply and lucidly, understandably with emotion, but without hysteria. Sympathy began to flow their way from a normally sceptical press.

The first mother to tell her sad story was clearly upset; Mrs H described the knock at the door that woke her and her invalid husband at seven o'clock. She told how the police and social workers came into her house, and said they'd come to remove the children. She asked them why; they said it was because they had information that the two children had been sexually abused.

They were told nothing else; only later they heard the abuse was supposed to have taken place outside the family. If this was indeed the case, why were those children ever removed from their own home at all? Apparently there were no allegations at that time against these parents.

Their house was not searched at the time of the dawn raid; they were not driven away to a police station for questioning. They were followed around the house as they washed and dressed, but the social workers were stopped by Mrs H from going upstairs to get the children up. She promised violent action if the social workers put one foot on the stairs, and went to get the children up and dressed herself, accompanied and watched by a policewoman; then her eight-year-old daughter and nine-year-old son were taken away without further comment, but the policewoman encouraged the children to take some clothes and other possessions with them.

Next to speak was a father. Mr T is a tall, distinguished looking man, who, with tears in his eyes, told the same story – at least in the beginning. When he opened the door and his house filled with strangers, he was told they had the right to take his two children away. They were, he said, holding papers in their hands. These were warrants to remove the children, and to search the house. Bemused by what was happening he moved to go to the bathroom, and was immediately grabbed by two police officers.

'These people,' he said, 'had come into our home and had the right to restrain us. They had the right to take away our children, and there was nothing we could do about it.'

His wife, followed by social workers, went to get the children, already disturbed by the commotion. Their twelve-year-old son had crept downstairs and listened at the door. He had seen children taken from his class at school the previous November. He knew why so many people had invaded his home so early in the morning. He wanted to run, but found himself surrounded. His eight-year-old sister was calmer; she, too, knew what to expect.

These children were permitted to wash and dress, and even to take with them pendants their father gave them. After they had gone, he said, he couldn't remember whether they'd said goodbye; whether they had wrapped their arms around their children for a last loving embrace. He could only remember their mother telling them through her tears to be strong, and to have faith.

This father, an Englishman – like the other parents involved in this affair – then told what happened next. The phone rang and he moved to answer it, but the flex was pulled out of the wall by the police before he could speak. The house was painstakingly searched, room by room, drawer by drawer, cupboard by cupboard. Every leaf of every book was turned – and this in a quiet, studious family with many hundreds of books.

Every child's drawing was scrutinised, every paper and letter read. He and his wife could not move around their own home without a police escort. Nor were they allowed to contact their family doctor or anyone else for support or advice.

Mr T told the packed public hall at St Margaret's Hope that he had brought his family to Orkney to get away from the pressures of much of life in mainland Britain. He said he and his Jewish wife both did a lot of reading and writing. She also wrote poetry, often reflecting the healthy sexuality of a woman in her early forties who enjoyed a fulfilling family life. The police, he said, removed all that poetry.

They also took private papers relating to the large South Ronaldsay family Mr and Mrs T had been trying to help, and a library book written by a social worker on sexual abuse. They removed a detective novel by Dame Ngaio Marsh because it bore the picture of a goat on the front cover. They took a number of other unrelated objects, and finally they took both Mr and Mrs T in separate police cars, driving them very fast over the adjoining islands where the sea lapped the famous barriers, to the mainland. There, they too were questioned continually for almost six hours.

Mr T said the police were perfectly civil in their questioning. He was treated with consideration. Although they didn't actually mention it, he said, he began to realise they were looking for suggestions that rituals had taken place, that he and his wife were part of it, and that their children were victims. The police asked if he and his wife went pot-holing. He was distressed when they asked about his wife's fidelity, and in her turn Mrs T was accused of infidelity as she was interrogated separately from her husband. She was told she had had intercourse with an eight-year-old boy.

Mr T said they felt unclean, violated. He voiced their torment at knowing their children would be medically examined without consent and without any familiar face being present. They agonised over how their children would feel in unfamiliar and hostile surroundings as they, too, were interrogated.

A mother, Mrs B, was next to stand before the sea of faces gathered in St Margaret's Hope village hall. Her courage was twofold. Her husband, working in England, was not with her, and she had had to go through the agony of 27 February alone. Quietly she gave her version of events, often struggling to hold back the tears. At ten to seven that terrible morning she had woken her elder daughter, a thirteen-year-old who, with her eleven-year-old sister, was sleeping in a caravan just outside the front door of the family home. This was their temporary bedroom while the house was being renovated. After waking the older girl, her mother went back into the house to finish her coffee, and almost immediately heard first one, then several other cars go speeding up the lane past the door. This family lived between two farms up a narrow, deeply rutted country lane. Their neighbours in the farm beyond were also raided that morning, and to get to that farm the police cars had to go past Mrs B's front door. Some of them stopped outside it.

With a terrible dread, she knew at once what was about to happen and ran to the caravan door to prevent her unwelcome callers from entering it. She was surrounded by police and social workers. Inside the caravan her elder daughter was pushing at the door to come out. Her mother opened the door and took her in her arms, still in her thin nightclothes, and screaming. She still barred the way so the social workers could not get to her younger daughter.

'You're not taking my children – over my dead body – there's no way I can allow you to take my children' she shouted. She was told they had a warrant and there was nothing she could do about it. The older girl cried 'Don't let them take me, Mummy,' and they stood together on the doorstep for several minutes, until a policeman gently reminded Mrs B that her daughter was getting cold in the dreary February morning. She ushered the girl inside and sent her to the bathroom. The thirteen-year-old locked herself in. Assuming everyone else would go into the house, too, her mother followed her.

Mrs B told the police and social workers that she must telephone her husband in England; she must tell him what was happening to his children. She was not allowed to make that call or any other. She was not permitted to call a solicitor, or minister of the church, or even a friend. She had to cope completely alone. To the hushed hall she described her feelings of real fear, of helplessness and panic.

She remembered her younger daughter, aged eleven, was still in bed in the caravan and ran out to discover that the child had been wakened and dressed by social workers, and was already in their car. She ran to the car, leaned in and touched her head. 'Don't worry, be strong, we'll do what we can,' she told the frightened child, 'and the hand of the Lord will look after you.'

To the end of her life, said Mrs B, she would never forget the look on her daughter's face. She looked petrified, but was blindly obeying the social workers, and silently appealed to her mother to help her. Her mother described her as a dog waiting for the next command, and all she wanted to do was hold out her arms and say 'Come here', but she was completely powerless to do anything at all.

This child is asthmatic. Her mother feared the trauma of being snatched from her could bring on an attack, and ran around frantically trying to find both the inhaler and the child's tablets. She was told by the social workers not to worry, they'd look after her. But they did not know beforehand that one of the children they were about to take suffered from asthma. They had made no checks with the families' doctors. In the end the mother discovered the girl had one of her two inhalers. The tablets she found later and took them to the Social Work Department to be sent to the child. In all the time the child was away she never received them.

By this time the youngest member of the family, an eight-year-old boy, had got out of bed and was clinging to the bannisters at the bottom of the stairs. The social workers had gone to his room and woken him, and he followed them downstairs. He had heard what was happening to his sisters, and was very distressed. His mother was talking to the police at the time, but she insisted on dressing him herself, and told everyone not to touch him. She tried to make light of the situation by telling the child this would be better than having some teeth out, which was planned for the following day.

She knew she had to let him go, but after buttoning him into

his coat, she wrapped her arms tightly around him, crying almost
hysterically. She knew, too, she had to try and reassure the children,
and struggled to control herself. Two policemen forcibly took her
arms from around her son, and led him out to the car to join
his sister.

The only child left now was the eldest girl, still locked in the
bathroom upstairs. Her mother ran upstairs, followed closely by a
policewoman who hadn't left her side for a moment since they'd
arrived. A policeman attempted to open the bathroom door with a
crowbar, denting the wood. The girl was so frightened by this that
she opened the door herself. Then, as they dragged her away, she
clung to the handbasin.

As the elder girl was taken out to the car, with police and
social workers on either side of her, she turned round, touched
her mother's arm and said 'Are you all right, Mum?' This was the
final straw for Mrs B who broke down completely at the thought
that her daughter could still think of her mother when this horrible
thing was happening to her.

The children were allowed no breakfast, the younger two were not
permitted to go to the bathroom, and none of them was allowed to
take a single personal possession, not even a teddy bear or something
to be a link with home.

After the children were driven away, Mrs B was taken back into
the house and told the police had a warrant to search it. As in the
other houses, they were thorough. They even searched between the
sheets and under the mattresses, and gave no answer when she asked
what they were looking for. She would, she said, have given it to
them, if she'd known what it was. At that point she was cautioned,
and she remembered words like 'lewd' and 'libidinous behaviour'
being used. She heard mention of six months' imprisonment, and
was terrified that she'd be locked up for doing nothing.

Having cautioned her, the police were ready to take her away from
her South Ronaldsay home for questioning. She insisted on feeding
the cows first, and also on changing her clothes before she went.
She sensed their impatience. They had issued the caution, now
they were anxious to get on with the questioning, and they only
had six hours from the time of the caution in which to hold her.
The policewoman, still in Mrs B's words, 'stuck like glue' while she
washed and dressed. Then she, too, was driven at very high speed
to a police station on mainland Orkney for interrogation.

The questions centred very much on her neighbours. Who were they? How long had they been in Orkney? What were their characters? Had they belonged to the 'flower power' era? What sort of music did they like? What did they use the trailer for? (These people are farmers; they have a variety of trailers, with a variety of different uses, all quite normal on a farm.) The questions continued: Did Mrs B's neighbours use the quarry on their farm, and if so, what for?

Then the local minister became the subject under discussion. They wanted to know if he had ever grown a beard? This question, said Mrs B, seemed to be of particular significance, but she had felt unable to make any sense of it. Without support or reassurance from anyone, she faced the seemingly endless questions.

She herself had been named as wearing a white robe – and was asked had she ever done so. She told them that apart from a white jumper she never wore the colour at all. She had grey hair and didn't wish to emphasise the fact. She began to piece together the line of questioning. They were after signs of ritual abuse.

From Mrs B's house and the caravan, police had taken away fourteen cassette tapes. Some were of classical music, one a relaxation tape she used herself, and the rest an assortment belonging to the children.

In the middle of the afternoon, at the end of the six hours' questioning, Mrs B was driven back through the dark, dreary day, and dumped outside her garage door. She had difficulty finding her house key in her pocket, but when she did manage to open the door, she ran into the house and up the stairs screaming wildly for her own mother. Her mother had been dead for twenty years. There was no comfort, no solace there.

There had been silence in the crowded village hall when she finished. Tears were rolling down many faces. What was happening to people living ordinary lives in a so-called civilised society? Horror and outrage were deeply felt.

For the fourth family, Mr M told a similar tale. His fifteen- and eleven-year-old sons were removed from their home in the raid. Six policemen and five social workers arrived at his farm waving Place of Safety orders.

Mr M was not completely surprised. He and his wife had been involved in offering support and assistance to the family whose eight children had been removed the previous November. In doing so they

had met opposition from the authorities. Neither they, nor their two
sons, had any doubt why these people had invaded their privacy so
early in the morning. The children had also done their share, not
always wholly willingly, to help the family whose problems now
seemed so closely linked with their own.

Mr M was concerned, however, that the social workers who came
to his house had no means of identification. He checked the police
ID cards, and finally had to accept that the police would vouch for
the social workers. They had all just pushed their way into the house,
and crowded into the small sitting room. It transpired later that the
social workers were all under instruction to have identification.

The fifteen-year-old heard his mother shouting. His mother
normally never shouted. He knew at once why she was doing
so now; he knew nothing else could have made her argue with
people on the farmhouse stairs at that time of day. A tall, strong,
mature boy, he considered 'doing a runner' and sprang out of bed.
On reflection, though, he decided it would be unfair to leave his
younger brother to face this alone, and he waited till they came
for him.

The two boys dressed, with a social worker looking on. Like
their three young neighbours, they were not allowed to take a
single personal possession – not a book, a teddy bear, a personal
stereo. Police tried to stop the older boy from saying goodbye to his
mother, but he did, anyway. Then he and his brother were driven
away into the cold February morning.

A slight variation in this household was that one social worker
stayed behind. He asked the parents to tell him about the children,
their tastes, their likes and dislikes. This was not done in any of
the other cases. No one knew about the little girl who suffered
from asthma; no one knew one family was Jewish and might have
different dietary requirements. No one, it seemed, knew anything
at all about the children they were uprooting so mercilessly.

After the two boys left the farmhouse, it was searched as system-
atically and thoroughly as the other houses. Police officers opened
boxes and bags in the attics where furnishings were being stored
for a new extension, and they went through the rest of the house
just as painstakingly. They scrutinised every cupboard, drawer and
corner. Every photograph was examined minutely, and some of these
caused apparent concern. One, of woods on Shapinsay, another of
the Orkney islands, had been taken by one of the children on a

school trip. Woods are rare in Orkney, and this one had proved an attraction. It was seen as sinister, however, and taken away.

A photograph of an older daughter of the family, then a student, had been taken in the small conservatory that leads into the house. Behind her, in the picture, were two gas lamps. The searchers went immediately to investigate, but only one lamp was hanging there. On enquiry they were told that the other had been lent to a local restaurant when it suffered a power cut. That lamp was later collected from the restaurant.

Again, every page of every book was turned; drawers full of letters were examined; children's drawings were inspected and some of these were taken away. Every item in the children's own rooms was closely inspected. Small coats with hoods, sent to the family from abroad, and long since grown out of, were taken away, together with twenty-eight videos. These contained recordings of many family films and television programmes.

Mr M asked for a receipt for all the items that were being removed from his home. The police said they would send one later. They never did so; it was not, they said, police practice to issue such receipts. The parents were not shown all the items taken by the police; nor were they able to oversee the systematic search of their home.

The police spent almost three hours going through the house and the farm. At the same time Mr and Mrs M continued with their daily tasks, feeding the stock, checking on cows ready to calve, assuring themselves that all, at least, was well on the farm. Every step they took was dogged by police officers.

At exactly 9.58 a.m. they were separately cautioned, and the words 'lewd' and 'libidinous behaviour' were used. Then they were bundled into separate police cars and driven, again at very high speed, to the Orkney mainland. They were taken to Stromness police station, and questioned persistently for the rest of the six hours allowed by law.

Their interrogators held a bunch of 'statements' in their hands. These, it appeared, were where the allegations had begun, and these, Mr M told the South Ronaldsay community, could only have come from some of the eight children who had been taken into care the previous November. The mother of those children was in the crowded hall with some of her older daughters. She stood up and told the meeting that she agreed. Whatever was being alleged against her neighbours must have come from statements made by her children in care.

Mr M continued. He said the questioning followed a similar pattern to the others. They were asked about playing music from a trailer, about dancing in a circle, about the quarry on their land. This is a Quaker family; they were asked about their religion and the form of worship they followed. Police eyebrows were raised when they described how they prayed sitting quietly in a circle. It was obvious to them that the word circle had sinister implications. Equally obviously the questioners were seeking confirmation of the rituals they believed had taken place; rituals that included real or simulated sexual acts between adults and children in the hours of darkness; acts that included ritualistic music, dance and dress.

All the families involved had moved from England to Orkney for a variety of reasons. They sought peace, tranquillity, and a chance to bring up their children away from many of the pressures of life further south. By this time they felt accepted into the local community, and part of it. Now, with no warning, no discussions, their children had been taken away.

Was this the price that these incomers to Orkney were to pay for befriending and attempting to support another family in trouble?

CHAPTER TWO

The Root of the Crisis

To understand how these families, regarded by their Orcadian neighbours as good, clean-living people, came to be at the centre of such serious allegations, it is necessary to go back a few years.

In 1986, a father of fifteen children then living in South Ronaldsay was jailed for physically abusing them. For some years the family had lived on the island of Rousay, where both the Social Work and Education Departments were actively involved with them, having been alerted by the school to concerns over the welfare of the children. The father, Mr P, also an English incomer to Orkney, had carried out various forms of abuse over a long period of time. One son, for example, was sometimes not allowed to sleep in the house, but was left out in the garden at night. The father regarded his children as his enemies. His wife, often pregnant with a new child, was unable to change things. Once the father was imprisoned, new and even more disturbing allegations began to emerge from the children.

This time, the stories were of sexual abuse, and again the father was the perpetrator. It turned out, however, that the police had heard about possible sexual abuse *before* the father appeared in court on the physical abuse charges. An older daughter had, in fact, told doctors in hospital of the situation. Some of the children had been talked to and examined, but nothing was found.

Following the new allegations against Mr P further action was taken. Some of the girls were examined again, and this time evidence of abuse *was* found. Their father appeared in court from prison, charged with the sexual abuse of his children. He was sentenced to another five years in jail on top of the two years for physical abuse he was already serving. The family changed their name to 'W'.

From the time of that trial, one of the girls, already disturbed, became more and more so. By December 1990 she had been described as psychotic by a doctor in the Sheriff Court. She had become a school refuser, and Orkney Islands Education Department

decided to offer her tutoring at home, and this was when one of the
families in the case in question entered the picture.

Mr M is a peripatetic teacher. At that time he travelled on a little
inter-island plane to the northerly island of Westray to teach for two
days a week; for a while he taught for two days on the island of Sanday
as well. His wife is also a teacher, and Orkney's Chief Educational
Psychologist, Peter Shearer, asked them to become involved with
the W family. They were to tutor the child who refused to attend
school, but there was to be more to it than that.

'Get in and socialise with the family,' Peter Shearer told Mr and
Mrs M. 'You're not just teaching one child, you're taking on the
whole family,' this being a family of fifteen children, some with
social and behavioural problems, and eight still of school age.

Mr and Mrs M and their family befriended Mrs W and hers.
They offered tuition for the child who was refusing school, and a
social relationship which meant inviting the W children to play on
the farm. Here the M family continued the socialising process begun
at home with the children by Mrs W and a family friend after their
father was imprisoned. The friendship of the M family helped to
reinforce the efforts being made by the children's mother to create
a more stable background for her family. It was a friendship that
was to have terrible consequences.

As well as teaching, Mr M and his wife run a farm on South
Ronaldsay. Since they moved to Orkney in 1984, they have invested
a great deal in the farm, and work very hard at all hours. They
breed cattle and sheep, and their two younger sons help them. So
do their two older children, a daughter and another son, when they
are on holiday from university. Theirs is a close, loving and caring
family. They have room within it to welcome strangers and make
them friends.

This is what they did for Mrs W and her children. The children
were invited to the farm to play, to swim with other local children
in the now infamous quarry. That quarry, it should be said, is not
much more than a small hole in the ground with banking around it.
It contains a spring, and the youngsters have a lot of fun there in
the Orkney summer. They shout and lark about, the way growing
children have always done.

It was into this carefree atmosphere, where hard work and a loving
family impose their own disciplines, that the W children came. It was
here they experienced a taste of what normal family life could really

be like. It was here they learnt to abide by the rules of the house, and the safety rules over the use of the quarry. It was here they learnt to trade rides on their ponies for rides on other children's bikes. It was here they learnt to communicate on a more civilised basis than they were used to.

Others in the local community joined in with this socialising process, offering hospitality and a chance to mix with adults and children on a day-to-day basis. The minister and his wife offered the freedom of the manse, and the children started to go to Brownies, Boys' Brigade and Sunday school.

Not all the local families were at ease with this situation. Indeed, the two M boys themselves were not totally happy at first at having these initially undisciplined children visiting their home and generally being around on a regular basis.

Mrs B, just down the lane from the farm, described them as rather wild. She wasn't keen on her three rather quieter children being involved, and asked them to return home from the farm if the W children arrived to play. Inevitably, of course, there were occasions when all the children did play together, and they all knew each other well.

The young Ws began to make some progress socially, and Mr M said he felt all was going well. The Education Department appeared to be delighted with what they were doing with the family, and any materials required for teaching the one girl were supplied eagerly and promptly.

'We were the good guys then,' said Mr M. 'We were sorting out a problem family for them.'

Between them they taught the girl from February until June 1989. Then, just before the end of the school summer term, all the W children under the age of sixteen were taken into care by Orkney's Social Work Department. The uplift came amidst allegations that the younger children were now subject to abuse from older siblings. These allegations were never tested, and after a month the children were returned home, and the mother resumed the care of her large family. With the father in jail, and teaching and socialisation in hand, why was it necessary to use emergency procedures?

The children were taken from Orkney to mainland Scotland under Place of Safety orders. While they were there, complicated moves were made to try and have these orders extended by a Children's Panel Hearing in Inverness, but the case was sent back to the

Orkney Panel. It was their responsibility to deal with Orkney children.

Orkney Children's Panel, however, with Mrs Katherine Kemp at that time the Reporter, recommended social work help within the family. At the very least they wanted a home help once or twice a week, to assist this mother with fifteen children to look after. The panel also hoped that a tutor/carer, possibly an older man, could be assigned to the family to teach the child Mr and Mrs M had taught, and to provide some sort of male role-model. Mr M was no longer available as he had started a new contract to teach four days a week in the northern isles.

The panel recommendations were never acted upon. Orkney Islands Council Social Work Department refused to implement the independent decision of the Children's Panel, and blamed the Reporter for allowing them to reach it.

Several hearings were held, and as a teacher involved with the family, and as someone who'd been asked officially to 'socialise' them, Mr M was asked to give information to the Children's Panel. He was asked about the girl's progress and about her ability; he was asked for his impressions of the family. He told them that there was definitely good progress on all fronts.

Mr M was very impressed by the Children's Panel system that, he said, seemed to take so much time and trouble to listen to, and about, the children. He felt doubly glad he'd brought his own children to live in Scotland where such a superior system of child care existed. The panel members appeared to him to be very patient, very fair, and very thorough. What he didn't know was that the local authorities were taking a very different line. They portrayed the family as hopeless, without possibility of improvement, and wanted the children kept in care.

To complete their picture the local authorities had to discredit Mr M and his work with the family. Another witness described how a member of the Education Department attempted to play down Mr M's contribution by strongly criticising his character at the Children's Panel Hearing. He undermined all the work that had been done by Mr M with the W family. That official now holds a very senior post in the Education Department.

The panel decided that the W children should be returned to their mother. On their return to Orkney, however, the Social Work Department put them into the Camoran Children's Home in Kirkwall. The family solicitor threatened to sue the council for not carrying out the panel's decision and allowing the children to go home. They were finally released a week later and sent home under a supervision order. This meant that a social worker would call regularly to check on their progress, and to make sure that everything was all right. The social worker regularly assigned to the case seemed to call when most of the children were at school, so he was unable to judge their progress at first hand.

By now, with the termination of Mr M's role as tutor to the girl who refused to go to school, she was receiving no education at all. She then took matters into her own hands. Daily she went to the M's farm and asked Mrs M to teach her. Mr M by this time was away on the outer islands for four days a week. The Education Department didn't like the situation; they did not co-operate with advice or materials as they had done in the past, and in fact the island's Director of Education accused Mrs M of 'acting illegally'. In spite of this, the tuition continued until the October school break.

In October, the Orkney weather demands that the cattle have to be brought into cattle-sheds for the winter. That October, when the M's cattle were brought in, it meant that Mrs M had to spend up to five hours a day working with them as Mr M was away teaching for much of the time. Mrs M no longer had the time to devote to the girl who sought schooling for herself.

It was then that the local community got together and offered to help. Mr T, the father of two of the children taken away in February 1991, had been a lecturer before he brought his family to live a quiet and peaceful life on a beautiful island. He offered to tutor the girl, but after trying to teach her for a while, gave it up as he considered she was unable to focus on what she was being taught. Mrs T also tried to work with her, but found her very vague. Mrs Jan Mackenzie, wife of the Reverend Morris Mackenzie, the local minister, also offered to help. She had trained as a teacher and did supply teaching for Orkney Islands Council. Music and art teaching were offered by other local people, and they all ferried the girl around from one tutor to another, so she wouldn't miss anything. It wasn't an ideal situation, but it was educational provision of a sort, and local people thought that was better than nothing at all which was what the girl was being offered at the time by the authorities.

This continued until Christmas. In January 1990 the Education Department provided her with a new tutor.

Meanwhile Mr and Mrs M's concern over the way the authorities handled the case of the W family grew. They wrote many letters on behalf of Mrs W. They wrote to the MP for Orkney and Shetland, Jim Wallace; to Winnie Ewing, Member of the European Parliament for the Highlands and Islands, and to the Scottish Office. They began to realise that many procedures had been wrongly carried out in the management of the case, in particular that the Social Work Department were not implementing the decisions of the Children's Panel.

Mr and Mrs T were writing letters, too, and the Reverend Mackenzie was voicing his concern. They all wanted to see the case of the W family properly administered. They all felt injustice was being done, and that the local authority was ignoring the rules. In December it was arranged, without his knowledge, that Mr M would lose two of his four days' teaching in the outer isles at the end of the academic year. His work on Sanday was to be taken up by a teacher who already lived there, and had been doing the job before Mr M was sent there. Why, Mr M wanted to know, had he been sent to Sanday at all? Was it possible he was being distanced from the large family they were trying to help? He believed Orkney Islands Council found him an annoyance. Mr and Mrs M still continued to take an interest in the family, to offer them friendship; they still wrote letters, and sought answers to a number of questions on proper procedures.

Once a new tutor was appointed for the girl who refused to go to school, Mr and Mrs M drew back a little. At last, they thought, the Islands Council was beginning to get things right.

Then, in March 1990 the Reporter to the Orkney Children's Panel, Mrs Katherine Kemp, was locked out of her office and suspended from duty by the Chief Executive of Orkney Islands Council, Ron Gilbert. At around the same time the Chairman of the Panel, Philip Cooper, suddenly resigned. A conscientious man, he took his duties very seriously and was renowned for his independence and fairness. Some say he was 'encouraged' to resign. Eileen Laughton, a former Panel Member who respected him greatly said he was worried about the pressure that was likely to be put on him if he didn't toe the local authority line. A senior teacher, he was, of course, employed by the council, and he also had six children of his own.

According to Eileen Laughton, a Panel recruitment drive at the time seemed to acquire the services of a number of people who would not be disposed to argue with recommendations from the Social Work Department. It began to look as if the way was clear for members of the department to take any action they chose, in the sure knowledge that their decisions on how to deal with problems such as the W family would be implemented.

On 31 October of that year, 1990, the annual review of the case of the W family was held by the Children's Panel. By this time Gordon Sloan, a Reporter from Strathclyde Region, had been brought in to do the work in Orkney, as the islands' own Reporter, Mrs Katherine Kemp, was still under suspension, and the details of her case were lying on the Secretary of State's desk in Edinburgh.

At the review, Panel Members who knew the children from the previous case were called for the Hearing. The children themselves appeared, and after a second summer spent playing at the M's farm, and becoming 'socialised' by contact with that family, it seemed they had made some progress. They had been accepted, too, into various youth organisations, and by some of the local community. Many others, however, (and it's believed this group included Orkney Islands Council) would have liked to see the family leave South Ronaldsay altogether. The Panel considered lifting the supervision order, but didn't. They did lift a restriction order that had prevented the children being taken out of Orkney, and this was to prove very significant.

The girl who was being tutored out of school, and was, it must be remembered, a very disturbed child, had made a number of allegations to her teacher. These implied that one of her younger brothers, an immature boy who hadn't reached puberty, had been sexually abusing both herself and a younger sister.

She further alleged that an older brother had been doing the same. This brother had been working in Derby for some considerable time. What the girl was suggesting was probably impossible, but it seems the logistics were never checked. She alleged, too, that she had an illegal relationship with her mother. *None* of these allegations was referred to in the Hearing on 31 October.

The very next day, on 1 November 1990, this girl was taken into care by the Social Work Department. Significantly, it was the day before her sixteenth birthday and she was the only one of the family to be taken into care that day.

Five days later, on 6 November, her younger brothers and sisters – seven in all – were also taken away. Social workers went to the primary school in St Margaret's Hope, a brand new open-plan building, and removed them from there in front of the other children. Some struggled and cried and tried to escape, which caused a great deal of distress to their watching schoolfriends. The youngest child in the family, not yet old enough to be at school, was on a shopping trip in Kirkwall with one of her oldest sisters. She couldn't be found when social workers called at the family home.

News travels fast in Orkney. It's the sort of place where you can hardly sneeze without your neighbour and their neighbours, and the people in the next village, feeling the breeze.

The news of the school uplift reached the two shopping in Kirkwall before they set out to travel the twenty miles or so back home. Instead of going home they fled, with their mother, to the manse, and sought a kind of sanctuary with the Reverend Morris Mackenzie and his wife Jan. After they were finally discovered to be there, the minister pleaded for them to be allowed to stay the night, and guaranteed they would be at the Children's Panel Hearing in Kirkwall the next day.

They were, and a heart-breaking scene took place. The youngest child was torn, screaming, from her mother, and taken away. It was even too hard to take for the traditionally cynical press. One young male reporter left in tears and said he would not cover such a case again.

The eight children from that one family, taken from Orkney in November 1990, remained in care somewhere on the Scottish mainland. It was many weeks before their mother learnt where they were. For six months they received no letters, cards or phone calls from other members of their family or from friends. They did not even receive presents their mother and other people had sent them for Christmas. The youngest child believed her mother to be dead. The children were subject to regular 'disclosure therapy', and it is from these disclosures that the allegations against the four South Ronaldsay families were made.

When the W children were removed amidst allegations of sibling abuse, there were those in the community who did not dispute this. Some believed this was entirely possible, but continued to support the family by writing letters denouncing the procedures carried out by Orkney Islands Council. Mr and Mrs T questioned whether family counselling might have been a better way of dealing with a very complicated situation, or at worst whether an interdict could be placed on the older boys in the W family. They asked for all the recommendations for a carer, and home support to be implemented.

After they were removed, Mr and Mrs M resumed their efforts on the family's behalf. They composed a letter to the Social Work Services Group, a department of the Scottish Office, and to the Local Government Ombudsman. The letter alleged serious breaches of the Social Work Act, and offered five witnesses prepared to testify in a court of law to that effect. The letter also specified details of non-observance of the Scottish Office guidelines. That letter was in draft form, ready to be checked by lawyers, then typed out and sent off on the morning of 27 February 1991. That was the morning when the police and social workers came to take their children away; the morning when seven other children were also removed from their homes in what many people saw as 'revenge' on the part of the local authority.

CHAPTER THREE

Practices and Procedures

None of the leading players in this drama doubts the need for child protection. No one, either in Orkney or beyond, denies that child abuse exists; some say that the sexual abuse of children is rife in today's society. Others look for evidence of rituals and declare that ritualistic and satanic abuse is happening much more often than most people are prepared to believe.

The initial shockwaves that devastated the Orkney island community of South Ronaldsay following the removal of the nine children from these four families, turned very quickly to disbelief and then to anger. How could the authorities treat children in this heartless and dispassionate manner? How could they say, as they all did, frequently and sanctimoniously, that everything they had done was in the best interests of the children? How could the best interests of the children be served by tearing them from their beds and flying them away from their island home to be completely separated from everything dear and familiar. How could those managing the case totally ignore so many guidelines issued by the Scottish Office and others to give assistance, particularly to social workers?

Principles of good practice and procedure are laid down in two main Scottish documents. One is 'Effective Intervention: Child Abuse Guidance on Co-operation in Scotland'. The other is 'Code of Practice – Access to Children in Care or Under Supervision in Scotland'. Also referred to by many, although it is an English document, is 'The Cleveland Inquiry Report' by Lord Justice Butler-Sloss. This was presented to parliament in June 1988.

'Effective Intervention' was produced in Scotland in the same year. It was sent to directors of social work and others in local authorities in 1989. The document contains sensible and sympathetic guidelines for dealing with children and their parents in cases of abuse. Following its publication, regional and island authorities in Scotland were advised to produce new local guidelines that would be relevant in their areas. Many of them have done so; many continue to monitor and amend them as situations change.

Orkney Islands Council have never developed guidelines of their own. Neither did they abide by the Scottish Office guidelines; they carried out the dawn raids and removed nine children from their homes in an emergency operation without reference to any of these documents. It took some time for such an admission to emerge. The Director of Social Work, Paul Lee, was asked constantly by pressure groups, by the press, and indeed by Social Work Committee Councillors, for a copy of Orkney's own guidelines. The answer was always that a copy would be made and forwarded. This never happened. At last, one very persistent councillor received a copy of 'Effective Intervention', and eventually Mr Lee admitted there was no Orkney document. There was, however, no statutory obligation upon the Council to produce one.

What lies within the published guidelines is very relevant to the actions taken by Orkney Islands Social Work Department. Or not taken, as the case may be.

The authorities did not approach the local general practitioner in the village of St Margaret's Hope, the village on South Ronaldsay which became the focus of allegations of abuse. Dr Richard Broadhurst is doctor to all of the nine children who were removed. Neither he nor his partner was asked about family backgrounds, possible problems, or whether any of the children had been presenting any unusual symptoms. He said he would have expected to be consulted. He could have helped to clarify issues, could have done some investigations of his own, and would have then alerted the relevant department to any problems. An excuse for not consulting him was given much later – as part of this close island community, he may also have been involved.

A director of social work in another part of Scotland, consulted about the actions his authority would have taken in the same set of circumstances, said that before even considering removing children from home, he would have consulted family doctors. This, he agreed, would have been his first move had such a case landed on his desk, and he would have talked, too, to the local health visitor. Next, he said, he would have talked to the schools.

The social workers in Orkney did not go to the children's teachers before the removal of the children to find out if there were any problems at school. They didn't ask if there had been any strange behaviour patterns, difficulties with school work, or inexplicable changes in the usual conduct of any of the children.

Following the children's departure, the Social Work Department did go to Miss McLeman, the Head Teacher of the primary school in St Margaret's Hope. They asked her for 'pen portraits' of the seven children who were pupils at the school. These were described by the parents later as inadequate and often inaccurate. The children's class teachers were not consulted. For the two older children, both pupils at Kirkwall Grammar School, the same sort of 'pen portraits' were supplied by guidance staff, and were also considered by the parents to be woefully inadequate.

Normal practice in cases involving the suspected abuse of children, whether physical or sexual, is to hold a multi-disciplinary case-conference. Those present might include the social work case workers, doctors, teachers, district or community nurses, playleaders, and anyone else directly involved in a family where such problems were suspected.

No multi-disciplinary case conferences were held prior to these children being taken from their homes. The people who knew them and their families best were never consulted. The purpose of such case conferences is to consider all the relevant information, evidence and opinions resulting from an investigation and assessment.

The 'Effective Intervention' document says: 'Parents should be informed or consulted at every stage of an investigation. Their views should be sought on the issues to be raised prior to a case conference to afford them the opportunity to seek advice and prepare their representations. They should be invited, where practicable, to attend part, or if appropriate, the whole of the case conference unless, in the view of the Chairman of the conference, their presence would preclude a full and proper consideration of the child's interests.'

This exclusion is generally held to be applicable when a criminal prosecution is in prospect. In the Cleveland Report, however, Lord Justice Butler-Sloss does not consider this should prevent the attendance of parents. Social workers, she says, have a primary responsibility to ensure that the case conference has information relating to the family background, and the parents' views on the issues.

It is also important that parents should be present to clarify and challenge information that comes before such a case conference. These Orkney parents were neither informed nor consulted about anything at all. Nor were they informed of the outcome of any conference that might have been held. The guidelines say they should be so informed, and it should also be confirmed in writing.

The 'Effective Intervention' document states that the investigation of child abuse or risk of abuse *always* requires social as well as medical assessments. *No* home or social background reports were prepared either before the Orkney snatch or afterwards. The Social Work Department had no information about these four families, and in particular about the nine children taken from them.

In the Cleveland Report, the British Association of Social Workers is reported as stating that it is absolutely essential that those involved with the family should conduct the fullest assessment of the family background. The association maintains that a full family history has proved over and over again to be of vital importance.

They believe that it is necessary to look at the parents individually. The parents' relationship must be examined, the vulnerability of the child or children assessed, and their situation within the family. They should look, too, at the family's social situation, their contacts with the extended family, and their perspective of the events which set the referral in motion. In other words, the investigating authorities should know everything there is to know about such a family, both from inside that family, and from contacts outside.

Social workers in Orkney, it seems, even ignored the guidelines laid down by their own association. The families were never asked for their own perspective of the events or the allegations. None of the assessment work was ever carried out.

The voluntary organisation, PAIN – Parents Against Injustice – visited Orkney within a fortnight of the removal of the children. This organisation had worked with parents in both Cleveland and Rochdale. PAIN is a national charitable organisation which offers advice, counselling and support to parents, children, extended family and professional carers who claim to be the victims of procedural and/or legal injustice within the child protection system. They had worked widely within the English system, but less within the Scottish one, with its lay Children's Panels, and less emphasis on the courts.

Two members of the PAIN organisation went to Orkney to prepare a report on the events as they had happened up to that point, and to compare the reality with the guidelines. They stated that none of the background reports or assessments had been carried out, and stressed that these are fundamentally necessary in order to determine what is in the children's best interests.

PAIN'S main concern was that, as with both Cleveland and Rochdale, a social services department of a local authority had failed to carry out good practice in the execution of their work. Sue Amphlett, director of the organisation, having studied the Scottish Guidelines, outlined nine main areas where Orkney Social Work Department had failed to implement proper procedures and practices.

The failure to carry out assessments and to inform and involve parents has already been covered here. An even more drastic failure was to deny any form of access between the parents and the children from the time of their removal. The children were away from Orkney for five weeks. In that time they were totally isolated from any contact with their parents, or with anyone else they knew or who cared about them. The two older children had no legal advice. Although minors, they had legal rights of their own, and could have engaged a solicitor, but they were never informed of these rights. A solicitor, engaged by the parents to ask these children their views before the Hearing on 5 March, was not allowed access to them.

'The Code of Practice: Access to Children in Care or Under Supervision in Scotland' states that 'authorities should put a high priority on arranging and maintaining close links between the child and his parents (and other close members of the family) while he is in care'.

In Orkney not only did the parents not see or have any access to their children, they were not even allowed to communicate by letter or telephone. Older siblings living in mainland Scotland were not permitted to see or communicate with their younger brothers and sisters, even though they were in no way involved or implicated in the allegations that had been made against the parents.

A rabbi from Glasgow, who had never met the parents at all, wanted to visit the Jewish children. He was not allowed to do so until just before they returned home, and too late for Passover. Quaker Elders visited the Director of Social Work in Orkney, Paul Lee, and the Chief Inspector of Police in Inverness on 5 March. They asked for access to give spiritual support to the Quaker children. The parents asked for access to be given to the Salvation Army, Baptist or Church of Scotland ministers, but all such requests were refused. No spiritual support was allowed to the isolated children, even though, as one parent bitterly commented, 'even prisoners are allowed this'.

Around three thousand letters and cards were sent to the children while they were away from home in a campaign resembling those organised by Amnesty for political prisoners. Grandparents, schoolfriends and neighbours all tried to write to the children, to send messages of love and support. None of these were received by the nine children isolated by the events.

The children were away over Mothering Sunday; they could not send cards to their mothers. In an expression of community sympathy many local children in South Ronaldsay made and sent cards to the four devastated mothers. The sideboard in the M's farm living room was covered with Mothers Day cards, but on that day none of them were from Mrs M's own two sons. The following week, both these boys managed, with the help of those they were staying with, to send cards to their mother. They were the only ones allowed through in the five weeks the children were away from home.

The children were still away over Easter. From all over Britain letters and cards poured in to Orkney's Social Work Department for the nine children in care. They came from complete strangers, from Quaker groups, and from caring people who wanted to help in a small way.

There were hundreds of cards and postcards for each child. They started to get these the day they returned home. Then they came back to the families in batches, sometimes several hundred at a time. Many of the cards were dated two months before they were received. Some, known about through enquiries from the senders, were never 'found'.

Easter eggs were sent, too. Ordinary, commercially-packaged Easter eggs made by all the well-known chocolate companies. These never reached the children until they went home, either, but the wrappings were torn and removed, and the eggs closely inspected. Some were smashed, some had holes cut in the top. What did the social workers expect to find? An old and much-loved teddy bear was sent by Mrs M to her younger son. It was never received, and only returned some considerable time after the children went home. It had been opened up and re-stitched in a different coloured thread. Teddies sent by Mrs B to her children were never received and never returned.

In the Scottish 'Code of Practice' document it further says: 'It is important that parents feel involved in the admission process and, wherever possible, in pre-reception planning. Emergency admissions will require particular care if parents are to be reassured from the outset that they have a continuing role in their child's life'. These parents were allowed no role at all. It may be surmised that, had these children been away as long as the Rochdale children were, this state of total separation would have continued. As it was, the five weeks seemed like a lifetime, and it was one that took its toll of parents and children.

Paul Lee, Orkney's Social Work Director, consistently said that what had been done was in the best interests of the children. At one point he indicated that it was in the best interests of the investigation. He repeatedly stated they needed to get on with the 'disclosure' work as quickly as possible. He stood by his Department's actions, and said they had had no option but to do what they did, in the way they did it. He denied that guidelines were not followed. He eventually suggested that Orkney had used Highland Region's guidelines, but the procedures used did not, in fact, comply with even these guidelines.

Mr Lee was fully supported by the Chairman of the Social Work Committee, Councillor Mairhi Trickett. She went on record to reassure parents that no children were taken with a revenge motive. This was already being discussed widely as a possible motive for the action that Orkney Islands Council had taken. Mrs Trickett said that the police and social workers were 'in receipt of information' which made it essential to take these nine children to a Place of Safety. Not to have taken action, she said, would have laid her department open to a charge of negligence. Asked by many, particularly those in the national and local press and media, about the need for an early morning raid to remove the children, she said there was no right time to take children.

After school, Mrs Trickett suggested, they would probably be engaged in other activities; at bedtime perhaps only one parent would be at home, and the children would be tired. At least between seven and eight in the morning, she said, the whole family would be together, and the children would be rested. This, she thought, would make it easier for them to cope with a very traumatic situation. She further condemned the press use of the words 'dawn raid', describing it as an emotive term.

In contrast to the statements of the parents, Mrs Trickett maintained staunchly that both the children and parents were kept informed of the situation and what was happening. The director, Mr Lee, she said, had written to the parents, inviting them to come and talk. She said too that all questions about their children to the department would be answered courteously. The families received no explanations, and received no written information regarding the procedures or the law. They felt they had been abused themselves; they felt impotent against the power weighed against them; they felt they had no way to fight back.

At no time were there satisfactory answers to questions about the lack of background reports. No reasons were given as to the lack of information the social workers had gathered about the children; why they didn't know about one child's asthma, another's forthcoming dental treatment, or that Jewish children might have special dietary requirements. At no time could the department justify why they had not allowed a rabbi to visit the two Jewish children in the mainland foster homes, or permitted Quakers to visit the two Quaker children. Can all these refusals really have been in the best interests of the children?

The Orkney parents were never informed by the Islands' Social Work Department of their own legal rights and the statutory powers, duties and roles of the agencies involved. Because of their involvement with the W family, some of them were by this time quite familiar with the Scottish Office 'Effective Intervention' document. They had read and understood it even before their own children were removed. They tried to make the Social Work Department follow its guidelines, but some of the parents believed the social workers didn't know much about the document at all. This was later discovered to be the case. The department had a copy of the document, but its staff were not familiar with its contents.

'Effective Intervention' states that parents need to know the reasons for the professional concern about their children. They need to be informed of the statutory rights, duties and roles of the agencies involved, and their own legal rights. The Scottish 'Code of Practice' document states again that all such important information should be confirmed in writing.

There was talk of taking this whole matter to the European Court of Human Rights. One former Orkney councillor suggested this course of action to the Isles Euro-MP, Winnie Ewing. In 'Effective Intervention' the role of the European Court is outlined. The document states: 'It is important that parents and/or carers be informed about the basis of an investigation or intervention. Agencies need to be aware that the European Court of Human Rights, in finding the United Kingdom Government to be in breach of articles six and eight of the European convention of Human Rights in recent child care cases, cited failure to involve the parents in decision making as a factor in their judgements.'

It continues by saying that parents should be consulted at every stage of investigation. The Cleveland Inquiry Report endorses this by stating that they should be informed and consulted whether the investigations are medical, police or social. They are entitled to know what is going on, and to be helped to understand exactly what steps are being taken.

The Orkney parents weren't told about any complaints procedures either. The 'Effective Intervention' document says all agencies should ensure there are clear procedures for parents to follow, and that information about these procedures should be provided. The Orkney parents were left so uninformed, they believed that all their rights had been removed.

The PAIN report also sharply criticised the fact that children were, once again, taken from their beds. This action by the Social Work Department only served to compound the trauma the children were experiencing being removed from their homes and families at all.

The report concluded by stating that Orkney Islands Council failed to implement good working practice as required by the Scottish Office. It drew comparisons between the events in Cleveland, Rochdale, and now Orkney, stating that there had been a consistent failure – if not an outright refusal by Social Work Departments – to carry out proper investigations, pooling of information from the families and all the professions and services involved with them. Not to do so means that they are not truly working in the best interests of the children.

Councillor Mrs Mairhi Trickett continued to insist that everything they had done was in the best interests of the children. Social workers and the police would not have taken the action they had, in the way they did, unless they had been absolutely sure there was a reason.

She was scathing in her criticism of the PAIN organisation, too. She questioned their qualifications and their authority for conducting an independent inquiry into the working of her department, particularly as their report contained no input from that department.

The PAIN representatives had tried repeatedly to see Paul Lee, the director of the Social Work Department. They were repeatedly told he was too busy, and when finally, at the eleventh hour, they were granted a meeting, some sort of communication problem caused Mrs Sue Amphlett and her associate to be sent from one building to another and then to wait for some time in the wrong one, until they had to leave to finish the report in time for the news conference they had called.

With reference to the PAIN report, however, Mrs Trickett commented on the guidelines which the department had been accused of breaking. They were just that – guidelines, she said, and each case had to be dealt with on its individual merits. PAIN, along with parents, lawyers and many others involved in the Orkney case, wanted to see those guidelines given the full backing of the law.

Another aspect of the procedures followed by Orkney Islands Council caused great concern in many quarters. This involved the role of the voluntary organisation, the Royal Scottish Society for Prevention of Cruelty to Children.

The RSSPCC played a leading role in the Orkney affair. They were contracted in by Orkney Islands Council to deal with the cases. They were already involved. Their social workers were undertaking the 'disclosure therapy' with the W children already in care in mainland Scotland. These were the children from whose statements the allegations had developed against the four families.

RSSPCC social workers were involved in the dawn raids on 27 February; it was mainly to suit their convenience that the children were flown away from their island home to an unfamiliar environment. There they could be near to RSSPCC centres where interviewing could take place; and in those centres the Society's social workers repeatedly interviewed and questioned the nine children they had taken away.

When two of the Society's officials visited Orkney for consultation with the Social Work Department, the Orkney grapevine ensured that everyone in South Ronaldsay knew they were there within a very short time of their arrival. The officials were personally invited by the Action Committee representing the families to go to South Ronaldsay and meet the parents. They were asked to talk to them and find out for themselves about the families who had been thrown into such torment; they were asked to talk about the children and about their lives at home. The RSSPCC officials refused, saying they were on a 'special mission'.

They did talk to the media, however. Raymond Starr, Director of Child Care and Family Services, confirmed that his agency had been called in because Orkney Islands Council did not have the resources to deal with a case of this kind. It was a unique case, he said. He was asked about the secrecy involved and the necessity for the early morning raids, and he answered that both the Society's and the Council's major concern was for the interests and feelings of the children, and that necessitated confidentiality.

Mr Starr said the RSSPCC ensured that whatever the children needed in terms of safety and freedom, they would get. Only in this way would they be able to talk freely about what their experiences had been, and that would happen in a safe situation for them. But what about the children's primary need, that of contact with their families? Mr Starr said that had been weighed against other needs apparent in the case. He also said that talking to the parents was not an objective of the Society, nor should it be.

He refused to comment on whether his organisation was carrying out the interviewing or 'disclosure' work on the children; he merely reiterated that they were involved in offering their assistance in whatever way was required by the department who had contracted them.

'I *know*,' he stressed 'that within the rules of the Children's Hearing, that the best interests of the children have been weighed, and on the balance of probabilities, the appropriate action was the right action. I know that.'

Considerable disquiet was expressed over the Society's involvement in Orkney. A leading social work official in another part of Scotland said he was concerned that their staff were not properly trained, particularly in the field of disclosure work with children. It is a fact, however, that lack of resources makes the employment of this agency essential to some authorities.

Lawyers and supporters of the parents in Orkney questioned both the motives and the methods of this once trusted organisation. They called for an investigation into the RSSPCC's practices and procedures to be included in the terms of reference for the Judicial Inquiry which the Secretary of State announced would follow the legal proceedings.

They called, too, for a full investigation of Orkney Islands Council

Social Work Department, and of how social work officials managed to ignore Scottish Office guidelines in a case of such seriousness. In fact, they asked for the practices and procedures of all the agencies involved to be thoroughly scrutinised.

CHAPTER FOUR

Children's Panel Hearings

The disposal of almost all matters concerning children in Scotland is in the remit of the Children's Hearing system. The system was established in 1971, and has attracted the interest of many countries. It is a system which deals with children and their families away from the formality of the courts. It is a system which has become known as the 'Caring Hearing System' because people are listened to, and problems handled in a sympathetic way. It is a system where an independent panel takes the decisions, considering the best interests of the children.

In order to understand how the Children's Hearing system works, it is necessary to go back to the beginning and explain how it was established and how it was intended to operate. There are those who feel that after twenty years the general public should be familiar enough with the rules governing child care and child protection, but perhaps the occasion of the twentieth anniversary of the Children's Hearing system in 1991 was an opportune time to go back to its roots, to take a fresh look at how it works, and whether changes in society over twenty years point to the need for changes in the Scottish system of juvenile justice.

The Children's Hearing system grew out of recommendations made by the Kilbrandon Committee in 1964. The ideas behind the Kilbrandon Report were new and bold. They would set the treatment of children in trouble in Scotland apart from the rest of the United Kingdom.

It had taken three years for the committee, under the chairmanship of Lord Kilbrandon, to gather and consider evidence from a large number of bodies already dealing with child offenders and child neglect. Amongst these bodies there was a unanimous desire for changes in the laws that dealt with children. At that time all cases were dealt with through the law courts, the establishment of guilt or innocence, together with the imposition of punishment the prime aims.

The Kilbrandon Committee recommended that individual decisions should be made regarding the best measures for dealing with each child, and that these should be made separately from decisions about guilt or innocence. Their other recommendations were radical and changed completely the face of juvenile justice in Scotland.

They said the way children in trouble were dealt with should be decided by lay people. These people would not be trained in law; they would represent the interests, the social groupings and the nature of the community in which they would serve. They would, in fact, be local people, able to look at local problems with local knowledge, and deciding on that basis, individual treatment *in the best interests of the child.* It was important too, that these lay people should be from all walks of life, from different age and social groups, and comprise an even mixture of both sexes.

Kilbrandon said these lay people would form a panel within each local authority area. The size of the full Panel would vary with the size of the authority. Three members of that panel would conduct 'Children's Hearings'. These would be either two women and a man, or two men and a woman, and the Hearings would be conducted as informally as possible, in surroundings that would not be intimidating to children. The panel members would discuss in an informal and concerned manner all the relevant background information on the life of the child before them.

The committee then proposed the creation of a new official to work with the panels. Like them, this official would be a lay person, and would be *completely independent* of all other bodies and agencies. The official would be known as the 'Reporter', and could be drawn from the legal profession, from amongst social work professionals, or perhaps from administration. The Reporter would be the first person to whom any child referrals would be made. He or she would decide whether cases should go on to a Children's Hearing before the Children's Panel, or whether to take no further action.

To support the new system, the Kilbrandon Report recommended that a new type of social work organisation should be established. Statutory provision for this was made in the Social Work (Scotland) Act 1968. The Children's Hearing System itself was not established until April 1971, to enable the full reorganisation of social work to take place first. This then linked the juvenile justice system with the overall provision of social work. The *whole* child, within the context of family and school could be considered for the first time, not just the offence.

Kilbrandon didn't remove the courts and the legal system from the picture altogether. There would be no change in the common law regarding the responsibilities of the Lord Advocate. Exceptionally serious types of juvenile cases would still be heard in the Sheriff Court or in the High Court.

The Panel would also have recourse to the courts. If the grounds of referral were disputed by either parents or children, the Panel would have two options. They could discharge the case if they were convinced that there were no grounds by the disputing party, or they could take the case to the Sheriff Court for a proof hearing. This course of action continues twenty years after it was instigated by Kilbrandon.

At a Panel Hearing, the three panel members selected from a pool of serving members, one acting as chairman of the session, consider everything about a child's life. *The whole child.* This was an elemental part of Lord Kilbrandon's philosophy. The child's *needs*, not his deeds, he maintained, should be the test for intervention. He also insisted that parents were usually the best people to bring up their own children, and should be encouraged and enabled to do so wherever possible. Compulsory care, if absolutely necessary, should be in the child's best interest.

If the grounds of referral are accepted by both parents and child at the Hearing, the Panel looks at all the information that has been provided for them. This includes background reports from Social Work Departments, school reports, and information from any other specialised agencies who have been engaged in helping the child or the family.

If the grounds for referral are denied, then the Hearing either refers the case to the Sheriff Court for proof, or discharges the disputed ground.

At the end of the Hearing the Panel makes one of three decisions. They may continue the case in order to gain more information; they may make a supervision order, involving the child living at home but under regular supervision, or being sent to live elsewhere in the care of others; or they may discharge the referral altogether.

The Kilbrandon Committee stressed the importance of training for the lay people who would become Panel Members. After selection by a local Children's Panel Advisory Committee, new members are confirmed by the Secretary of State for Scotland. Then a rigorous initial training period begins.

New members must undertake a stretching programme of lectures, discussions, group work – including role play, visits of observation to special schools and assessment centres, meetings with people who work with the Hearing system, and study. There is a lot of reading material to get through and absorb, and there are cases to attend as an observer before a new Panel Member finally makes up one of the three actually hearing a case.

Even when new members are regularly taking their place on Panels, the training continues into every aspect of children's lives, into care, physical, mental and sexual abuse, criminal activity, and ways of dealing with the variety of cases that come before them in the course of their work.

Throughout the training, which does vary a little from region to region, new members are encouraged to question everything. They are constantly reminded that they are an independent body, and the decisions they will be called upon to make must be based on their own findings from the information put before them. They are told they are not there simply to implement the wishes of social workers, or police, or anyone else. They, and they alone, have the right to dispose of a case involving a child.

The Reporter is, of course, a very important figure within the system. As already stated, he receives the first referrals. These may come from many sources; from police, social work, other agencies, parents, or indeed from any private individual who may be concerned about a child. The Reporter makes the initial decisions about whether to proceed any further with a particular case.

The Reporter, although not necessarily a lawyer, must ensure that the Hearings stay within the legal framework. He or she must provide the Panel with all the available information, making sure the social background and other reports are to hand. One of the parents involved in the Orkney case asked Paul Lee, the Director of Social Work, if he was going to prepare a social background report on her family. He replied that it was the Reporter's job to ask for one. This, apparently, was not done, but in the majority of Panels this report is expected to be before the Hearing and is provided by the Social Work Department without a request from the Reporter.

The role of the Reporter during a Hearing is described as legal adviser and clerk. He or she will note the proceedings and advise members of the Panel on procedural matters and on points of law where necessary. The Reporter should not direct the Panel regarding their decisions.

There may be three reasons why court proceedings follow the Children's Hearing. Either, as has already been explained, the grounds for referral are disputed by the parents or the children, or a child may be unable to understand the grounds through age or mental incapacity. Thirdly, the parents themselves may appeal against the decision of the Panel in the disposal of a case. In any case it is the role of the Reporter to present the evidence and argue the case before the Sheriff.

Before taking a decision on whether to take a case to a Children's Hearing, the Reporter has to consider the reports from all the appropriate agencies. He or she will then discuss the case with all those deemed necessary in the best interests of the child. At this point the Reporter does not have to account to anyone else. Although financed by the local authority, the appointment of the Reporter must be approved by the Secretary of State for Scotland. No Reporter can be removed from office, asked to resign, or be employed in another capacity without the consent of the Secretary of State.

Another important element in the system is the Children's Panel Advisory Committee, known as the CPAC. Here again the Secretary of State must approve the appointment of the chairman and members. Members of the Advisory Committee are drawn deliberately not only from those who have experience of the system, for example, former panel members, but also from people who have not previously been involved in the Children's Hearing system at all.

The CPAC, as this advisory body is known, is responsible for the recruitment of panel members in their area. It also monitors the performance of serving panel members and makes recommendations about re-appointment at the end of each panel member's term of office. The Advisory Committee forms part of the checks and balances which make this Hearing System so unique, and which, since its inauguration in 1971, has kept many thousands of young people out of court.

In Orkney a number of events concerning the operation of the Children's Hearing system caused great concern. Doubts arose over the competence of the system to cope with cases of such magnitude.

Concern was expressed by lawyers, families, councillors, and even Orkney's re-instated Reporter, Mrs Katherine Kemp, over the relationship between Orkney Islands Council's Social Work Department and the Children's Panel.

Some panel members believed that decisions taken by the Children's Panel were not implemented by the Social Work Department, and therefore threatened the independence and integrity of the Panel. The suspension of Mrs Kemp for over a year with no reasons being given by the local authority, caused grave misgivings in Orkney.

On 27 March 1990 Mrs Kemp, herself a former social worker, was suspended without any prior warning by Ron Gilbert, Chief Executive of Orkney Islands Council. The locks on her office door were changed to prevent her from gaining access. She was denied any opportunity to appear before councillors in order to appeal against her suspension. Her only recourse was to make a formal appeal through her lawyer.

During much of the period leading up to this time the Panel had been considering the case of the large South Ronaldsay family whose father had been imprisoned – the family of fifteen children who so badly needed a positive and sympathetic solution to their problems.

Following Mrs Kemp's suspension in March, in April 1990 Orkney's Chief Executive, without any direct authority from Orkney Islands Council or councillors, and without notifying Mrs Kemp, applied to the Secretary of State for consent to dismiss her from her post as Reporter to Orkney Children's Panel. Mrs Kemp's lawyer, Robert Shaw, believed that, since the law which governs Reporters and their duties provides that a Reporter may not be removed from office except with the consent of the Secretary of State, this would also prohibit suspension. This would make the action of Orkney Islands Council illegal.

The Secretary of State called for written submissions from the parties involved. In May 1990 Mrs Kemp received a copy of the submissions of the Chief Executive. These contained a number of allegations that had never been raised with her at all. She made full answers to all of them. She was still awaiting a date for the hearing of her appeal against her suspension. The Chief Executive had been notified that her lawyer would be on holiday on 11 July so this date should be avoided. On 4 July Mrs Kemp was told that the hearing would take place on 11 July.

There followed correspondence between Mrs Kemp's lawyer and Orkney Islands Council's Director of Administration and Legal Services, Rowan McCallum. He indicated that he would introduce whatever evidence he thought to be appropriate, regardless of whether such evidence had formed part of the reasons for the suspension or not. When Mrs Kemp's lawyer, Bob Shaw, asked what line of questioning he would use, Mr McCallum angrily refused to reveal what evidence would be produced. Mr Shaw said he had never been spoken to in such a manner by another lawyer. On behalf of Mrs Kemp he objected to this denial of the rules of natural justice. On 6 July Mr McCallum cancelled the hearing, which he had no authority to do. Mrs Kemp strongly protested against his action.

Then the Chief Executive made further submissions to the Secretary of State, who was at that time Malcolm Rifkind. These submissions contained further allegations which had not been previously raised. Again these were received and responded to by Mrs Kemp. She asked the Secretary of State to hold an inquiry at which parties could be heard and witnesses examined.

No further date was set for Mrs Kemp's appeal in Orkney, despite monthly requests to the Chief Executive, Ron Gilbert, to the Council Convener, Jackie Tait, and to the Director of Administration and Legal Services, Rowan McCallum. Eventually, in a letter to Mrs Kemp's lawyer, Mr McCallum offered 24 December 1990 as the only free date for a hearing, but added it was not the most suitable date. None of the councillors on the Appeal Committee would want to attend an appeal on Christmas Eve. Mrs Kemp was left with no alternative but to accept that no hearing could take place.

In a statement issued on 8 April 1991, Bob Shaw said there was little confidence that Mrs Kemp's case was being fairly dealt with. Justice was neither being done nor being seen to be done. In this view he was strongly supported by Councillor Spencer Rosie of Orkney Islands Council. He had fought hard over the year of her suspension to have her case dealt with speedily, and to get at the truth behind the allegations. He said that councillors had no idea what was going on, and could only rely on the advice of the council's officials. Mr Rosie, who has since resigned from the council, had contacted Orkney and Shetland MP Jim Wallace and the Scottish Office to try to discover the cause of the delay in settling the matter. No satisfactory answer was ever received to that particular question.

Another Orkney councillor, Ian MacDonald, believed he was

barred from serving on the Social Work Committee because of his continued support for Mrs Kemp. He said that certain officials and a councillor were determined to get rid of Mrs Kemp because of the demands she was making, and had consistently made during her whole period in office, for the improvement of child care in Orkney.

Councillor MacDonald remains on the council, outspoken when he sees the need to question the activities of this very singular local authority. Councillor Spencer Rosie, much to the loss of the community he served, resigned from Orkney Islands Council in April 1991, due, he said to pressure of work, and the wish to spend more time with his own growing family. The council could ill afford to lose a man of his calibre, who fought for openness and honesty and against secrecy in its affairs.

In the meantime there had been two significant events which affected Mrs Kemp's case. A new Secretary of State, Ian Lang, had replaced Malcolm Rifkind at the Scottish Office. And on 27 February 1991 nine South Ronaldsay children were taken into care on Place of Safety orders. In the opinion of many people, Gordon Sloan, the Reporter on attachment from Strathclyde Region to replace Mrs Kemp, did not inspire trust or confidence, and there was a renewed call for the Secretary of State to deal with her case as soon as possible.

On Tuesday, 23 April 1991, one year and twenty-seven days after her suspension, the Secretary of State refused to allow her dismissal. In a short statement Mr Lang rejected Orkney Islands Council's attempt to sack her. He said he had made a full examination of the submissions made to him by the council and by Mrs Kemp. He concluded that the council had not made a sufficient case to justify dismissing their Reporter. She would have to be re-instated, and her suspension rescinded.

There was no easy end to this situation, though. Orkney Islands Council did not give up without a fight. They didn't just acknowledge gracefully that they'd been beaten, or perhaps even that they had been wrong, and welcome their Reporter back. Instead a special meeting of the full council was called to decide what action to take following the Secretary of State's decision. Mrs Kemp and her solicitor were refused access to that meeting, and were only told of the outcome some time later. A vote was taken on whether she should be re-instated, and by a very narrow margin it was agreed that she should. It is hard to see what else they could have done in view of the Secretary of State's decision.

First, though, two Scottish Office representatives, a retired Children's Panel reporter, Alan Finlayson, and an under-secretary to the Secretary of State, travelled to Orkney to review the Children's Panel and Social Work systems. Then it was agreed that Mrs Kemp would deal with all new cases. The Acting Reporter from Strathclyde, Gordon Sloan, who had filled in for the past year, would continue to look after the cases with which he had been involved. This included the case of the nine South Ronaldsay children who had been taken from their homes at dawn on 27 February.

The way back for Mrs Kemp certainly wasn't smooth. Some members of Orkney's twelve-strong Children's Panel threatened to resign if she was re-instated. They sent letters to the council's private meeting to try to block her return. One of the letters was from Jean Robertson, who chaired the Panel at one of the Hearings involving the nine children. Another was sent by the Chairman of the local Children's Panel Advisory Committee.

Another member of the CPAC in Orkney is the Chairman of the Social Work Committee, Councillor Mrs Mairhi Trickett. It is, however, usual for the Social Work Chairmen to be on these Advisory Committees. It is also known that two of the four panel members who complained about Mrs Kemp were employees of Orkney Islands Council.

During the case of the nine children who were taken into care in February 1991, one long-standing member of the Panel resigned because of what she saw as the deterioration in the Children's Panel Hearing system in Orkney since the suspension of Mrs Kemp. Mrs Eileen Laughton, a passionate believer in the Hearing system as established following the Kilbrandon Report, said her conscience wouldn't allow her to keep silent any longer. She had tried to put matters right in the proper manner from within the system, but that hadn't worked, and she believed the Children's Hearing system was at risk in Orkney.

A member of the Panel for twelve years, Mrs Laughton had written in November 1990 to the Secretary of State for Scotland, expressing her concerns about the deterioration of the system in Orkney since the suspension of Mrs Kemp. Her letter was marked private and confidential, but instead of a reply from his office, she received notification from the Social Work Services Group that her

CHILDREN'S PANEL HEARINGS

letter had been passed to the chairman of both Orkney Children's Panel and the local Panel Advisory Committee. She was outraged. She wanted someone outside Orkney to take a long, hard look at what was happening within the islands.

The Acting Reporter, Gordon Sloan, on loan from Strathclyde, had no local knowledge. This, said Mrs Laughton, was completely against the ethos and proper practice of the system as established by Kilbrandon.

Mr Sloan had introduced Strathclyde procedures which she maintained had no place in Orkney. He directed the Panel Members, many of whom, she claimed, now believed their role was to follow his lead. Mrs Laughton said the Reporter had too much input into the Hearings themselves, and the Panel ceased to be independent. Mr Sloan took the Social Work Department's line, and the Panel were expected to follow it too. In other words they had become, in her opinion, a rubber stamp, and not an independent body making decisions for the authority to abide by.

There were other grounds for concern, too. At a Panel Members' training weekend at the Merkister Hotel at Harray in Orkney, on 10 November 1990, it is alleged confidentiality was breached by the public discussion of an ongoing case. It was just a few days after eight children from the W family from South Ronaldsay had been taken into care.

Later the Children's Panel Advisory Committee Chairman was informed about this alleged breach of provisions in the Social Work (Scotland) Act 1968 relating to the operation of the Children's Panel. It is believed no action was taken.

Mrs Laughton said that one of the reasons for Mrs Kemp's suspension was that she had objected to the Social Work Department ignoring the decisions of the Children's Panel. She had objected, and she was suspended. Mrs Laughton herself was told that her suitability as a Panel Member would be reconsidered at the end of her term of office in May. This, after twelve years' dedicated service to the system and all it represented to her.

Mrs Laughton resigned with much regret, saying as she went that Orkney Islands Council didn't appear to know what the role of the Reporter to the Children's Panel should be, and determined to make her concerns public.

Mrs Kemp resumed her duties as Reporter to Orkney Children's Panel on Monday 6 May 1991. On 10 May, Mrs W, the mother of fifteen children, eight of whom had been in care since the previous November, began an appeal against the care orders holding them. She and her lawyers arrived at Kirkwall Sheriff Court. So did the Acting Reporter, Gordon Sloan.

The mother immediately abandoned her appeal. She called for a formal review of the whole case by Mrs Kemp, now she was back in her post. She said she could not and would not continue to deal with Mr Sloan. It was impossible to speak to Mr Sloan, she said, and added that the Panel was never set up to be a court. She wanted the case dealt with in a proper and fair way; she did not, she said, expect Mrs Kemp to be more sympathetic, but she would be fair.

This incident seems to epitomise what is believed to have gone wrong with the Children's Hearing system in Orkney. Every region has its own methods of administering the system, and those of a huge area like Strathclyde are seen as being particularly inappropriate for an island community like Orkney. Yet these were the methods that were used in the South Ronaldsay alleged child abuse case.

CHAPTER FIVE

The South Ronaldsay Hearings

When emergency procedures are used to take a child into care, the Social Work Department has to obtain a Place of Safety order signed by a Sheriff or a Justice of the Peace. This is valid for seven days. In that time a Children's Panel Hearing must be convened, and the options assessed by Panel Members after considering all the information available.

The Social Work (Scotland) Act 1968 says that where a child has been detained in a place of safety, and the Reporter considers that the child may be in need of compulsory measures of care, he shall, wherever practicable, arrange a children's hearing to sit not later than in the course of *the first lawful day after the commencement of the child's detention* to consider the case. One of the parents involved in the Orkney case actually asked that the hearing should be held either that day or the next, to comply with this section of the Act. This parent, Mr M, had studied the 'Effective Intervention' document as well as the Social Work (Scotland) Act in his attempts to assist the W family. His request was not complied with, and the Hearing was not convened on the first lawful day after the children's removal.

In some areas, however, the 'wherever practicable' is translated to mean the seventh day, not the first. In many areas the Hearing is held on the first working day after the removal of the child. In Strathclyde, the region from which Gordon Sloan, the Acting Reporter in Orkney, came, it is the general practice to hold the hearing on the seventh day. This is certainly against the spirit of the law. It may be interpreted to be against the letter also.

The South Ronaldsay children were taken away on the morning of Wednesday 27 February. The latest possible date for the Children's Hearing was Tuesday 5 March, and that was the date chosen by Mr Sloan. The families were told to attend at half-hour intervals from ten o'clock onwards.

At a Hearing each parent and each child has the right to be accompanied by a representative. This may be anyone at all; it may

53

be a friend or relative; it may be a lawyer, although the Hearing is not a court and the lawyer has no legal status.

On the morning of 5 March, a Queen's Counsel was on his way from Edinburgh to speak as a representative for at least one of the families. The vagaries of travel to Orkney, however, including the fact that the scheduled flights were all booked up with journalists, meant he could not arrive in time for the ten o'clock start. He drove through the night to Wick intending to cross the Pentland Firth in a small private plane. Weather conditions precluded this, so he had to wait for the next scheduled plane from Wick to Kirkwall.

Lawyers for the families asked the Reporter if he would postpone the start time of the Hearing by one hour. He refused. They asked again, but he remained adamant. The Hearing would begin at ten o'clock. The lawyers sent an urgent message to their local MP Jim Wallace in the House of Commons asking for his help in the matter. Mr Wallace immediately faxed a letter which was delivered by hand to the Reporter, asking for one hour extra to be allowed. Mr Sloan then agreed to the postponement.

The QC, Edward Targowski, arrived a minute or two before the 11 o'clock deadline. He went quickly into the unpretentious terraced houses where the Children's Hearing offices in Kirkwall are situated. With no time for briefing, the Hearing got under way.

As he arrived, Mr Targowski was cheered by a large crowd of supporters and well-wishers, gathered to express their feelings about the situation that had drawn a cloud over their quiet island life. Many came from South Ronaldsay, and were friends and neighbours of the beleaguered families. Many more came from other parts of Orkney – Orcadians and incomers together creating an atmosphere of community and caring support. Many carried placards demanding the immediate return of the children. One Orcadian woman was quick to retort when asked why she was there.

'Can ye no read?' she demanded, holding up her poster. 'We want our children home. It's not fair they're away. They're in prison. What are the people supposed to have done? We don't know what they've done. I live no far away from two of the families; I can see both houses out of my kitchen window. There's no dancing going on up there. It's a wee community, everybody knows everybody.'

Another Orcadian was equally adamant that injustice had been done: 'We're here because we feel it's very wrong the way the bairns have been uplifted, and they're being treated quite like criminals really. If there has been any injustice, surely it should be the adults taken away and not the children.'

Many more spoke in that vein. They waited in a dignified and orderly manner outside the Children's Panel offices. There was no shouting, no hysteria; no mob tactics were used. Just quiet, controlled anger that the children should have been so arbitrarily removed to places where they had nothing loved or familiar, and no one to turn to. One supporter summed up the feelings of them all about the authorities who took them away.

'I don't know whether they feel that a satanic message can be sent in code by a parent to a child saying "I love you. Don't be afraid, it's all right, we're going to be with you sometime,"' she said. 'We feel very strongly about that and that the law should be changed for future children, so that they should be spared the anguish of separation and no contact at all.'

This was the children's seventh day away from Orkney. While they endured the loneliness of the enforced separation, the humiliation of intimate medical examinations, and harrowing interview sessions, their parents were at Children's Hearings in Kirkwall, starting the bitter fight for their return.

They began their fight by refusing to accept the grounds of referral to the Childrens Panel. This meant they denied that the allegations had any foundation at all. As a result, by law, the Hearing could not continue. As has been explained earlier, if the grounds of referral are denied by either parents or children, then the Panel has two choices. They can either discharge the case, or refer it to the Sheriff for Proof. The latter was the course of action taken that day.

The Panel, as had been expected, extended the Place of Safety orders on all nine children for a further twenty-one days. The children themselves were not present at the Hearing, as they had a legal obligation to be. The Social Work (Scotland) Act of 1968 states that 'where a child has been notified that his case has been referred to a children's hearing, he shall be under an obligation to attend that hearing in accordance with the notification'.

There are exceptions to this general rule, however. The Act continues: 'Where a children's hearing are satisfied in a case concerned with an offence mentioned in the Criminal Procedure (Scotland) Act of 1975, that the attendance of a child is not necessary for the just hearing of that case, or in any case where they are satisfied that it would be detrimental to the interest of the child to be present at the hearing of his case, the case in whole or in part, may be considered in the absence of the child.'

Children who are too young to understand explanations of their situation, or those who may suffer from learning difficulties understandably come into this category. So do cases where the trauma may be considered to be too much for the children. The youngest of the nine Orkney children was eight, the oldest fifteen. Their presence at the hearing had been dispensed with at a meeting of the Panel four days previously. The legality of that meeting was later questioned.

Before a Children's Hearing can proceed, it must be established that the grounds for referral to the hearing are clearly understood by both parents and children. They are explained by the Panel Member chairing the case under consideration. The only exception to this is where a child is incapable of understanding even a simple explanation of the grounds because it may be too young, or suffer from mental handicap. In such cases, the Panel would direct the Reporter to apply to the Sheriff for proof, unless they decided to discharge the referral altogether.

That was not the case in Orkney. The children here were all considered old enough by their parents to understand a sympathetic explanation of the grounds on which the Reporter had referred their case to the Children's Panel. The Panel decided in advance not to bring them back to Orkney for the Hearing. It was decided it would be too traumatic for them if they had to be flown away again afterwards. The children, in their foster homes in mainland Scotland, were not notified that the hearing was to take place. They were not told of the grounds for referral, and the case proceeded without them.

Although the Act does allow for children to be absent from Hearings under the circumstances already referred to, they should still be notified of the Hearing, and an explanation of why it is taking place should be given. These nine Orkney children were not informed; they were not told the Hearing was taking place; they were not given any sort of explanation.

Without any knowledge of the children's understanding of their situation and what was happening to them, the Hearing went ahead on the morning of Tuesday 5 March. The four sets of parents went in to the Panel separately, although they were to be treated as one case. In the small room the protagonists were crowded round a table. The parents, their representatives, the three Panel Members, the Reporter and two social workers. Four members of the press were allowed in at a time. There were so many journalists covering the Orkney story that they set up a pool system and took it in turns to go in.

It may come as a surprise to realise that the press have a right to cover hearings, although they may not, in any way, identify the children who are the subject of those hearings. They may report on 'four families', 'nine children', and give the reasons for referral, in this case the allegations against the parents.

At that first hearing in Orkney, on the seventh day after the removal of their children, the allegations of lewd and libidinous behaviour with ritual music and dance were read out to the stunned parents. Only five minutes before the hearings began they had been allowed to read these for themselves, and in the words of one family friend, the Reverend Derek Edwards, 'they were devastating . . .'

'To watch a mother's face as they're read back to her, even though she's read them for herself . . . the parent I was sitting with was shaking her head and crying. The reality that those things were being said of *her* was just beyond her comprehension, and for myself I have never heard something so outrageous in all my life.'

Mr Edwards was appalled at what could and had been done in the 'best interests of the children'. He joined the ever-growing group of people calling for a change in the law.

The parents left the Children's Panel offices looking tense and drawn. Their lawyers and supporters were grim-faced, although they said the hearing had held no surprises. The allegations were serious, and it had not been supposed that the children would be allowed home with no further action.

Outside in the street, still waiting in the cold wind were the friends, neighbours and complete strangers who had come to show their support for the families. The grandmother of two of the children sobbed when she knew for certain they would not be coming home. She had hoped against hope that somehow the Panel would realise that an enormous mistake had been made. She tried to be a strength for her daughter, but was overwhelmed by the enormity of what was happening to them all. The quiet sympathy amongst the waiting people was tinged with anger, and an Orcadian farmer voiced the feelings of them all when he said that bureaucracy had gone too far.

'What we want is the children back home. We want them looked
after in a caring way, and treated as children, not as bits of evidence
in some concocted case about satanism or something.'

The crowd, swelled by reporters, photographers and cameramen
from the local and national press and media, dispersed quietly
after the parents had left. A lawyer speaking for the families said
they would be appealing against the Place of Safety orders, and
that the appeal would be heard the following day in Kirkwall
Sheriff Court.

The courthouse in Kirkwall is in a particularly picturesque setting.
Set back from the road it faces the south wall of the magnificent St
Magnus Cathedral, and is separated from it by the road, and by a
peaceful park area and an avenue of trees.

These are the grounds of the seventeenth-century Earl's Palace,
described as being possibly the finest example of French Renaissance
architecture in Scotland. A ruin now, although much of it still stands,
adding to the beauty of the court surroundings. On the other side,
across a narrow lane called Watergate, is the original Bishop's
Palace, built in the twelfth-century to provide accommodation for
the splendid new cathedral. Rich in the history of Norwegian kings
and Orkney bishops, the palace ruins add their own poignancy to
the day-to-day dramas enacted in the handsome court building.

The friends and supporters of the four South Ronaldsay families
gathered outside the court on the morning of Wednesday 6 March.
Young children ran between the trees, their laughter an emotional
reminder of the children who weren't there. The raucous croaking of
the rooks amongst the tall sycamores and the ruined palaces seemed
an appropriate symbol of the ugly story that was unfolding in these
peaceful northern islands.

Again the parents were given encouragement and messages of good
luck as they went into the Sheriff Court with their legal advisers.
They were hopeful that things would go their way, but not really
very optimistic. The indications were that the Sheriff would uphold
the decision of the Children's Panel, and would support the Place
of Safety orders.

The Appeals were heard in private before Sheriff Principal
Ronald Ireland. Again the four families were heard individually,
but were treated as one case. Again they heard the allegations
against them on the basis of which their children had been taken
away. They left the court with no decision having been taken.

The Sheriff said he would give them his decision the following day.

This was announced to the waiting press and supporters by Dr Helen Martini, who was to play an important role in the fight to get the children home in the weeks that followed. A surgeon, Helen Martini was specialising in paediatric surgery when she gave it all up to move with her husband to Orkney. He is Dr Richard Broadhurst, GP to the four families embroiled in this case. Dr Broadhurst organised the first public meeting in St Margaret's Hope. Dr Martini chaired it, and now, a week later, she was becoming the spokesman for the families.

She stood on the steps of the court, and told the crowd gathered there that the parents had been told they would have to wait to hear whether the Place of Safety orders had been confirmed, or whether their children would be returning home.

The families, she said, had asked her to express their gratitude for the warm and caring support from everyone there; they were grateful, too, for the many messages of support and sympathy coming from outside Orkney.

Significant amongst these messages were those from the parents of Rochdale, who were that week awaiting a judgement in their own case. Their children had been in care for eight months. Their support and messages of comfort were all the more touching and meant a great deal to the Orkney families. The Rochdale parents said they were reliving their whole trauma along with the parents of Orkney.

Helen Martini joined the call that was growing louder and stronger for a full judicial inquiry. She stressed, too, that it should be held in public as families across Britain, from Cornwall to Orkney, were at risk from over-zealous authorities. As a doctor, she was more than well aware that children needed to be protected, and that abuse existed in many forms. She had seen it at first hand, treated children who were victims. As a citizen she was concerned that all too often social workers got an idea in their minds that ritual abuse was taking place, and then set out to look for it. The after-effects, though, were critical, according to Helen Martini.

'If, at the end of all this,' she said, 'no charges are brought, you've got nine traumatised kids. Who picks up the pieces?'

The next day, the loyal supporters, still holding aloft their banners and placards, were back outside the court in Kirkwall.

They hadn't quite known whether to be optimistic or pessimistic about the overnight delay, but they were adamant in their belief that none of these parents was capable of doing the things stated in the allegations against them.

Many of the supporters were eager to put their points of view to the waiting journalists. One young woman was particularly bitter about the system that allowed situations like this to develop. Some people were beginning to talk about retaliation or revenge against the authorities responsible. This young woman, however, did not believe this course of action would solve anything.

'I don't really think there's any point in calling for resignations of personalities. I happen to know that the Director of Social Work, and another of the senior social workers here, have moved here very recently. They didn't come here to be monsters, presumably. They came here to settle down and have a happy life. It is the system that is at fault here, and what I think is so appalling is the fact that children can be removed from their families and their environment without one single shred of evidence. I just think that will have to change, because it is creating utter havoc and misery in the community.'

Others, perhaps less charitable, did call for the resignation of the Director of Social Work, Paul Lee, and they believed the Chairman of the Social Work Committee, Councillor Mrs Mairhi Trickett, should also resign.

The mood of the crowd was turning to anger against those responsible for taking the children of South Ronaldsay away on what appeared to be very flimsy evidence, which had not been checked out through the appropriate channels. They were angry, too that the authorities, by their actions, had created such a feeling of real fear and impotence in Orkney in general, and South Ronaldsay in particular.

Sheriff Principal Ronald Ireland turned down the parents' appeal that Thursday morning. The Place of Safety orders were confirmed on the nine children, who would remain in care in mainland Scotland for several more weeks.

Leaving the court the families all tried to put on a brave face. One mother was distraught, the others said tightly that they had really not expected anything else. The lawyers, too, agreed that on the basis of what was before him, the Sheriff had no alternative. They were angry, however, that nothing more concrete than the allegations was available.

Two Kirkwall solicitors were acting for the four families. One of them, Alistair Bruce, told the waiting reporters that they would have expected any charges to have materialised by this time. It was over a week since the children had been removed, and both police and the Social Work Department had said they had made independent investigations which had led to their decision to take such drastic action. If this was the case, then there must be enough grounds for proper charges, said Mr Bruce, but every enquiry he made, to police, social work, or the Children's Panel Reporter, Gordon Sloan, was met with the same answer: 'Investigations are continuing.'

Mr Bruce said that the Social Work Director Paul Lee had been asked if the families' lawyers could have access to all the interviews and medical examinations of the children that were performed for the Social Work Department.

At this stage, too, he said, he and the other solicitor on the case, John Moir, had applied for legal aid for the four families. They needed to engage more senior and junior counsel to help them to fight what looked like turning into a very long legal battle. The fight was just beginning, but they would take whatever steps were necessary to win it.

CHAPTER SIX

Action Committee Starts Work

At the first public meeting in St Margaret's Hope, called only two days after the children were taken from their homes, a conscious decision was taken by the parents and the rest of the local community that supported them, to actively court publicity. In the face of their impotence to deal with the apparent all-embracing power of those ranged against them, the parents decided this was their only weapon.

These were articulate people, perhaps better able to deal with the press and media than some other families who have found themselves in the same position. Three families in Ayrshire, for instance, who had eight children taken away in a raid in June 1990; little was heard of their situation until *after* the Orkney case had been in the headlines for some time. Little was known, either, about the families of fourteen children taken into care in Aberdeen at around the same time as those in Ayrshire; they didn't look for publicity, speak to the press or generate such wide interest and public concern.

One of the Ayrshire families finally talked to some journalists in April 1991, some ten months after their four children had been removed. They protested their innocence, and referred to the fact that no charges had been brought against them. Their only contact with any of their children in all of that time was a monthly visit with their eldest child, in a bare room, accompanied by a social worker who vetted the questions each asked the other. One of the children taken from this family was only six months old at the time of removal.

The Orkney parents talked to reporters, appeared in photographs or on television with their backs to the cameras, and were unfailingly courteous, co-operative and welcoming. They must have longed for quiet and solitude, for space to shed their tears in private, or even to vent their anger, but none of them showed it in public.

Support in South Ronaldsay and the neighbouring island of Burray had grown so strong, and there was so much anger, that it was decided within the community that this strength should be channelled into action.

A second public meeting was called. This time it was held in St Margaret's Hope School, the newly built primary school in a commanding position on a hill above the village looking out over the sea. The hall was bigger than the Cromarty Hall in the village; it could accommodate more local people and more of the television cameras that by now were multiplying daily, along with their crews, reporters, producers, and the army of newspaper journalists and feature writers that by this time had gathered in Orkney.

Again the hall was full. The parents of the nine missing children sat together at the front. Leading the meeting were the two solicitors, Alistair Bruce and John Moir, together with Dr Helen Martini, and the Reverend Derek Edwards.

The last two had become prominent spokesmen for the families during the ten days since the removal of the children. Both had supported the parents during the Children's Hearing, and during the Appeal against the Place of Safety warrants. Both were vehement in their call for an Inquiry into the whole affair. Both were professional people with a vested interest in helping people – a doctor and a Baptist minister. Both had come from England to make their homes in unspoilt Orkney and had settled in the South Ronaldsay community. They were united, too by a common aim; they both wanted to do what they could to restore normal life in that community, to take away the fear and to see justice done.

At the first public meeting the Reverend Derek Edwards had said the Social Work Department was out of hand and out of control, and was able to make up its own rules in an arrogant and arbitrary manner. He also commented on the worrying growth of occultism in the nation. This, he thought, was a very disturbing reflection on modern life, and one which led some religious fundamentalists to search for satanism everywhere. He told the gathered community that he was committed to proving it was not active in South Ronaldsay.

At this second public meeting, the South Ronaldsay Parents' Action Committee was officially formed, with Helen Martini as Chairman, and Derek Edwards its Vice-Chairman. They were unanimously chosen by the community represented at the meeting, and their commitment was welcomed by the four sets of parents.

The two were the base of a formidable team, and they immediately declared their purpose was to give emotional, moral and practical support to the stricken families.

They were concerned about the cruel manner of the uplift of the children, and that such action had been taken without proper investigation. They were outraged at the suggestion, in the grounds of referral, confirmed by remarks made by the Interim Reporter in Orkney, Gordon Sloan, on 6 March that further members of the community were involved in the alleged abuse ring. The new Action Committee was determined that this allegation should be refuted. This comment by the Reporter now forms part of Sheriff Principal Ronald Ireland's written note in his ruling following that first appeal: 'Sloan to prove other members are involved'.

The Action Committee office bearers were confident that the characters of those adults accused, and those of their children, as well as the sort of events that could and did occur in their community, were better known to them than to Orkney's Social Work Department.

When they asked for volunteers to carry out the various tasks of such a committee, the offers came in promptly from all parts of the Hall. Two people would share the role of secretary; two more with a head for figures would take on the work of treasurer, an area which would necessarily assume vital importance with the huge legal costs that would have to be faced.

One local resident said he would organise free accommodation and transport for all visiting advisers and experts; another two volunteered to get a petition circulated throughout all the Orkney islands. Others offered to man phones, to work out rotas of helpers, and to provide clerical back-up for the two solicitors.

They came forward eagerly, offering what skills and abilities they had; farmers, a conservation adviser, a photographer, a botanist, a medical practice manager; most of them parents themselves, all of them becoming part of the support surrounding the South Ronaldsay families and determined to fight for them. Some were native Orcadians. Some had chosen these northern islands as the best place to make their lives, the best place to bring up their children. Their tranquil dreams broken, they were united in their resolve to repair the damage.

Once the tasks were allotted to the newly-recruited committee members, the meeting then turned its attention to the lawyers. It was clear that Alistair Bruce and John Moir would have to devote their entire time to preparing the case for the four families. It was clear, too, that they would have to do this together.

At the time the two solicitors worked for different law practices in Kirkwall. Each had to rely on the support and goodwill of his partners to be able to spend their entire time on the case of the South Ronaldsay children.

Now those same partners gave their blessing to the idea of the two solicitors moving out of their own offices, and setting up a temporary Law Centre where everyone involved could get together and fight for the return of the children; they would fight for justice, and ultimately a judicial inquiry. But where?

It was Alistair Bruce who came up with the idea. Just across the road from his office was a building with empty suites of rooms. The Orkney Tourist Board occupied much of the building, and faced onto the main road, and the Northern Studies Centre was in another part. It was right in the centre of the town, next to the Cathedral, and only two or three minutes walk away from the Sheriff Court. It would be a perfect location for the work they had to do.

The building was owned by Orkney Islands Council, but there seemed to be no difficulty in securing a temporary tenancy. There was space enough for an office for the two solicitors, a room for the visiting advocates from Edinburgh to work in, and a meeting room for talking to parents, specialist advisers, and witnesses. The two lawyers told the meeting in St Margaret's Hope that the offices were ideal for their purposes. All that the rooms lacked were furniture and equipment.

They did not lack these for long. The following day, Sunday 10 March, Action Committee members and friends started to forage for office furnishings and equipment from anywhere they could get them.

By Monday the office was equipped with desks, tables, chairs, two word processors, telephones, a fax machine, a photocopier, and everything else needed for the efficient running of an office. That included a few old but comfortable easy chairs for the meeting area, plus a coffee table, a kettle and cups.

The room where the four senior and four junior counsel from Edinburgh would work was fitted out with several very basic trestle tables, not perhaps quite what members of the Faculty of Advocates are used to working on, but Alistair Bruce described them as very resilient people. They were, he said, ready to muck in. Senior counsel Edward Targowski had already proved that when he made such an effort to travel to Orkney for the first Children's Hearing. His return journey had been even more dramatic, on a fishing boat, and for the first week he charged the families nothing at all. Alistair Bruce was sure the trestle tables would present the members of the Bar with no problems.

Many items were donated outright; many were lent for the duration, but everything was volunteered in one way or another. British Telecom responded with great promptness and had two telephone lines and a fax line installed on Monday. It was almost a miracle. The Legal Centre was up and running and ready for business. Work started there in earnest on Tuesday 12 March. The solicitors moved in, volunteers answered phones, typed documents, and novices learnt to operate the computers and word-processors.

The support from the Parents' Action Committee continued to grow. Rather tentatively at first, volunteers came forward to work the word-processors; another manned the phone continuously from that first day until the office finally moved out of its temporary accommodation in the middle of May. Other committee members were in and out of the new Law Centre, holding meetings, planning strategy, contacting people with wide experience of the sort of situation they found themselves in, and collating information.

This coming and going caused its own problems, though. The two solicitors needed peace and space to work on what was a very complex case. It became obvious that the Parents' Action Committee needed to find somewhere else to carry out its own work. That somewhere wasn't long in materialising, either. An empty house just a mile or two outside St Margaret's Hope village was put at the disposal of the Committee. It was on the market and it was a grand gesture by the owner – one that was much appreciated by the parents of the nine children, and by the Action Committee that had come together so promptly to support them.

The house, called 'Quindry' is an ugly, flat-roofed box-shaped building, which resembled a factory unit rather more than a home. Its saving grace, however, was a windowed passage-way with spectacular views of the sea and the land beyond. Here was office space and room enough for meetings. Here the hard day-to-day work of the committee got under way; there was always someone on hand to answer queries, provide information, make a cup of coffee.

Many newspaper journalists and reporters from radio and television found their way to Quindry. There they were received with unfailing courtesy and friendliness, and over endless cups of coffee checked out facts, co-ordinated information, and often interviewed Helen Martini or Derek Edwards.

The first big task the South Ronaldsay Parents' Action Committee set themselves was to circulate a petition round all the Orkney Islands. This was launched at the meeting at St Margaret's Hope on Saturday 9 March. To gather signatures for the petition was a formidable task indeed, because it had to be back in Helen Martini's hands by the following Thursday, so she could present it to No. 10 Downing Street on Friday 15 March. Six days to circulate a petition around the scattered islands. Nothing daunted, the committee members set to; they contacted friends and acquaintances on other islands, they studied ferry time-tables, and planned their campaign with a speed which matched that which had equipped the Law Centre.

The petition drew attention to the events in Orkney and the way in which the case had been managed; it asked the Prime Minister, John Major, to hold a public judicial inquiry into all the circumstances. It asked, too, for the working of Orkney's Social Work Department, and other involved Social Work Departments, to be investigated. And it asked for the Scottish Office Guidelines, and those in Lord Justice Butler-Sloss's Cleveland Report, to be made law.

In the end there were certain logistical difficulties in getting all the petition forms back from the outlying islands in time for Helen Martini's departure for London on Thursday 14 March. There were other problems, too. Certain teachers and other employees of Orkney Islands Council were, it was alleged, 'warned off'. They were apparently advised by people not named, that they should not take the petition round in their area, and they were also apparently reminded who they were employed by.

Many people, dependent on the council for their livelihood, refused to sign it. Others, on some of the more northerly islands, away from the emotion and strength of feeling in South Ronaldsay, were still murmuring that 'there's no smoke without fire' and speculating on what the parents of the nine children had been up to.

Helen Martini left Orkney on Thursday 14 March, and on the Friday presented the petition at the front door of No. 10 Downing Street. She had hoped for an audience with the Prime Minister, but

had to be content with the publicity of being there. At the same time
as the petition was being circulated, the Action Committee wrote and
widely circulated a letter that anyone, anywhere, could send to their
own MPs. It asked for their support in getting the law changed, and
the guidelines strengthened by law.

This letter was freely available at the opportunely-timed Scottish
Labour Party Conference, held that very week in Aberdeen. With
Shadow Cabinet Ministers, Labour MPs and Prospective Labour
MPs (including the candidate for Orkney and Shetland, John
Aberdein from Stromness) at the conference, the Action Committee
thought it was a good opportunity to make a lot of politicians aware
of the situation very quickly. Vice-Chairman Derek Edwards took
the opportunity to stress publicly the urgent need to make their
campaign a national one.

'We want every person in every part of the country to contact their
MP,' he said. 'They should write, phone and insist that Parliament
addresses this issue *now*. Not tomorrow, next week or next month,
but now.'

The Action Committee launched an appeal for funds. At the very
first meeting in St Margaret's Hope village hall they had asked for
monetary pledges, at the second meeting in the local school they said
it was time to call in those promises and start counting the cash. If
each family was to have the services of a senior and a junior counsel,
the costs would be enormous, and at that stage no one knew what
the position would be regarding the question of Legal Aid. Even
the solicitors could not say whether Legal Aid would be granted to
all or any of the four families. There had never been a case quite
like this in Scotland before.

The running costs of the Law Centre had to be met, too, and
all the incidental expenses of the Committee – phone bills, fax.
machine, petrol, stationery. Funds had to be found – and quickly.
Immediately the generosity of people within Orkney and much
further afield became apparent. Contributions came from all over
the United Kingdom. Large and small amounts were sent, pledges
were honoured. The work of the treasurers began in earnest.

Letters and phone-calls of support also came from every corner of
Britain. They came from young and old, from friends and strangers,
from church groups, and from families in Cleveland and Rochdale
who had been in the same position themselves. They even sometimes
came in person. Sylvia Hayes, an artist who had spent some time

painting in Orkney, came from Oxford to show her support for the four families.

'Once I'd learned about what had happened here, like so many other people I was absolutely staggered,' she said. 'Because I know perfectly well that there can be no sound evidence for such monstrous, silly accusations.' She went on to say that although she'd done what she could from her Oxford home, and encouraged her friends to do the same, eventually she just had to pack and go to Orkney.

'In the end I couldn't bear to be anywhere else,' she said, and added that if such practices had been going on in the islands as were alleged, everyone would have known about them.

'Of course they would. I would have known. I'm constantly out of doors, wandering along the cliffs, across fields. I've got to know so many people in the community, and I turn up at their houses any time at all. If such things had been happening, I would have come across them.'

Her sentiments echoed those of all the neighbours and residents of South Ronaldsay. The island is small, no homes are out of sight of others, even in the farmland; people know each other well and, as in all rural communities, they also know each other's business. No one there could believe that the allegations could have any validity.

With that strength of support coming from far and near, the South Ronaldsay Parents Action Committee launched itself into the mammoth task it faced. Each and every member of that committee felt changed by the events that had shaken their community. Each and every one felt threatened, felt their own families and peace of mind were at risk. They knew life in their island haven would never be the same again, but they knew, too, that their quality of life, free from fear of the authorities, was worth fighting for.

At the outset Helen Martini said the prospects of what they had taken on were daunting, but she had no doubts about what they could accomplish. The stakes were too high for doubts.

'In the beginning,' she said, 'when these children were uplifted, none of us had any idea what a national scandal we were dealing with. We thought it was a little local issue. It's not, it's a national scandal.'

CHAPTER SEVEN

Religious Mania?

In the midst of all the child-care and legal paraphernalia of hearings and appeals, another element in the whole affair caused distress. Because the allegations against the parents were centred around 'ritualistic' behaviour, the word 'satanic' began to be heard. During the police questioning on the first day, some of the parents were asked about Satan and satanism.

It's a subject that has gained momentum across the country in recent years. In Rochdale and in Nottingham it led to the removal of many children. It was used too, in Ayrshire. Some people believe that a sort of 'satanic hysteria' has invaded Social Services Departments across Britain. They believe that certain extremist Christian movements encourage workers in the social services to look everywhere for evidence of satanism. That 'evidence' can be bizarre and unlikely, such as the book with a picture of a goat on its cover taken from one of the Orkney homes, gas lamps and a Halloween mask taken from another, or a church minister's hooded funeral cloak.

The Evangelical Charismatic Movement has been described by religious correspondents as the fastest growing part of the Christian Church in Britain in the second half of the twentieth century. It is a movement that seeks to put the supernatural back into Christianity, saying God is supernatural, and so essentially Christianity is a supernatural religion. The movement began in America, and has been imported to Britain, bringing with it what many observers see as an obsession with satanism.

The Charismatics – part of this evangelical upsurge – feel they have been blessed with the direct gifts of the holy spirit, and one of the main ways in which this manifests itself is speaking in tongues. They see around them evidence of supernatural happenings. They say that God intervenes directly in a supernatural sense in what goes on in the world. By the same token, they say that the devil is actively at work as a supernatural force. They believe people can be possessed by demons, and that their role is to rid the world of such demons.

There is a great healing tradition within the evangelical Charismatic Movement, and those who adhere to it believe this healing is about seeking out the devil and ridding the possessed of this influence. They look for signs of his presence in all areas of everyday life. They talk about Satan being particularly active towards the 'end times' – that's the time when they believe Christ will return. Reading the scriptures, they translate this into the very near future. The Gulf War, for instance, fitted in quite precisely with some of the things forecast in *Isaiah* Chapter 13 about the destruction of Babylon. They also see the 'end times' approaching according to the *Book of Revelation*.

They see the signs of Satan everywhere, not just within dictators, and others widely acknowledged to be evil, but within individual people. Of a family where child abuse may be taking place, they will say that Satan has got into that family, and that there's some sort of evil force at work.

These Christians look for signs of satanic influence within families and encourage friends and colleagues to do the same. Since the mid-1980s when the satanic child abuse scare first came to Britain, it seems that many workers within Social Services in particular have been influenced by this thinking.

The Reverend Derek Edwards, Vice-Chairman of the South Ronaldsay Parents' Action Committee, and a Baptist Minister, voiced his concern that belief in large-scale ritual sexual abuse grows within agencies over the months and years. Once in the system, he said, it tends to perpetuate itself.

'People hear of it who know nothing of its origins. They receive information on it from people they trust, and whose opinion they hold in high regard. They see it as something that they, as the caring agencies, must be involved in if they are going to be doing a good professional job. Then, by a slow, gradual process, they get to a point where they expect to find ritual sexual abuse in the community in which they are working.'

Derek Edwards spoke, too, of the presence of Charismatics in Orkney: 'It's known that there is one social worker in this very small department who does belong to a Charismatic Christian Fellowship. The history of this Fellowship in Orkney goes back to the early 1980s . . . They've been living for the last ten years in an environment where they expect there to be a high level of occult activity in society. Coming from a background like that, I think those

views would make a Charismatic social worker highly sympathetic to
the views that he was receiving through the professional channels of
the social services.'

Another fast-growing religion in Britain at the moment is a
non-Christian movement. It is neo-paganism, or a revival of the
pre-Christian religion that was practised here hundreds of years ago.
In those times people worshipped according to the cycles of nature;
they held rituals at key points of the year, and in the minds of the
Charismatics they are very much associated with things like standing
stones. Orkney has a great many standing stones. The Charismatics
see direct satanic involvement in this revival, and say the neo-pagans
are devil-worshipping. The neo-pagans say this is nonsense, their
religion has nothing at all to do with the devil, because the devil is
an invention of the Christians. They claim they are pre-Christian
and good, not satanic and evil.

Nevertheless, the Charismatic Movement continues its relentless
search for evidence of satanic influence and there is a history of
an active Charismatic ministry in Orkney. The Orkney Christian
Fellowship was set up in the mid-1980s by a former Church of
Scotland Minister, Alan Cowieson, who had caused division amongst
a number of families while he was still Minister of the Evie, Rendall
and Firth Parish.

A summer camp held on the island of Rousay in 1990, in which the
Orkney Christian Fellowship was involved, is alleged to have created
a climate of fear and suspicion. Teenage girls returned from that
camp with stories of speaking in tongues and exorcising evil spirits.
Some of them had gone into trances, and questions were asked by
many worried parents. Some of the children needed psychiatric
treatment, and others received counselling by the orthodox Church
of Scotland clergy. Police enquiries were made into complaints from
some parents about the camp and the way it was run.

Many people involved with the alleged child abuse case in South
Ronaldsay think that the roots for believing that 'ritual' abuse was
taking place in the island were established at that controversial
summer camp. It is known, too, that Charles Fraser, one of the
social workers involved in the abuse inquiries in the family of
fifteen, and in the cases in question, is a member of the Orkney
Christian Fellowship. It is not known if the original allegations of
satanic ritual abuse came from this source.

It is certain that not one incident of satanic abuse has been proved anywhere in the world. An American child abuse counsellor from Illinois, Pamala Klein, was instrumental in bringing the scare to Britain. A self-styled psychologist specialising in child sex-abuse cases, she has now been discredited in both the USA and the UK.

Her influence, however, has been far-reaching. She 'diagnosed' one of the first British cases of satanic abuse, in Kent, in 1988 – over the telephone. Police found no evidence in that case and the child was returned to its parents. She developed courses on child abuse for senior police officers, and distributed a list of 'satanic indicators', or signs and symptoms to look out for, which have since been circulated to police forces and social workers across the country. In September 1989 she was instrumental in organising national conferences on child abuse – one at Dundee University – for social workers, police, and other child-care professionals.

Pamela Klein's crusade against satanism certainly helped to create the right climate for the prevailing tendency of Christian Evangelic Charismatics to step up their search for signs that Satan was at work. In some areas the Movement has become excessively exclusive. Members believe that *anyone* outside their particular way of looking at things is not a Christian at all – and this applies to groups such as Quakers. One of the families in the child abuse case in Orkney is a Quaker family.

The Charismatics are suspicious of anything they are unfamiliar with. If they suspect satanic influence amongst any group of people, they would also look with suspicion on anyone associated with that group, whether politically, socially, or on religious grounds. They would believe that all these people were caught up in this satanic net. A very dangerous piece of theology.

The Reporter, Gordon Sloan, inferred that the South Ronaldsay community were all involved in the abuse he believed to have taken place there. Was he suggesting there was a paedophile ring operating? Was he influenced by a growing tendency to look for ritual abuse?

People like Ms Pamala Klein would seem to have a lot to answer for. They have caused fear and suspicion and encouraged people to look for abuse where there is none, or to dress up actual sexual abuse of children with 'satanic' imputations. This may have completely the opposite effect to that intended. It may stretch credulity to the point that signs of real abuse are overlooked.

In Britain a Welsh woman, Maureen Davies, established the

Reachout Trust in 1983. She was part of an evangelical crusade that claimed many people were trapped in the occult. They said parents sexually abused their children as part of a satanic ritual, and that these practices were widespread.

The Reachout Trust prepared a paper on how to spot symptoms of satanic ritual abuse in children. It contained clear guidelines. Children who were preoccupied with the natural motions of their own bodies or who were difficult to toilet train were abused children; children who laughed when passing wind, or indulged in aggressive play were displaying the classic signs of abuse; destroying toys, harming animals, and being pre-occupied with death, were all stated to be symptoms of satanic ritual abuse.

The natural fears displayed by many children were turned into signs of abuse – such as fear of going to jail, fear of ghosts and monsters, fear of 'bad people' taking the child away, fear of being left with a babysitter. A clingy child was also an abused child according to these guidelines.

There were other stated symptoms, too, including singing or chanting odd songs – and what child has not spent time happily singing something totally incomprehensible to a parent? Another symptom is writing numbers or letters backwards – again a common enough thing to do when a child is learning to write, particularly if he or she is left-handed, or perhaps dyslexic; and probably most absurd of all, children who refer to television characters as real people are showing signs of abuse. Perhaps Maureen Davies and members of the Reachout Trust had never read any of the daily tabloid newspapers where the doings of soap opera characters are regularly reported as 'news'.

Maureen Davies advised social workers in Nottingham and Rochdale. She had earlier written a report called 'Facing the Unbelievable', which told of the ritual abuse of children. She has not been directly involved in the Orkney situation, but she did lecture on ritual or satanic abuse at a two-day seminar in Aberdeen in November 1990. The seminar was organised by the local Evangelical Union of Churches. It was directed at ministers and social workers, and it is believed that one Orkney social worker was invited to that seminar, as well as a Baptist minister who had helped to organise the summer camp on Rousay.

The Chairman of Orkney Island Council Social Work Committee,

Councillor Mairhi Trickett denied that any members of her department had ever been to any courses or seminars on the subject of ritual or satanic abuse. They had not been schooled in the symptoms of such abuse, but she told reporters that the abuse of children was such a terrible problem in society, that everyone should be on the look-out for it.

One minister of the Church of Scotland in Orkney had been growing increasingly concerned about the growth of extremism in religion. The Reverend Peter Brown, Convener of the Social Matters Committee for the Orkney Presbytery, began to investigate the actions of the Evangelical Charismatic Movement in Orkney, and whether any members of the Orkney Christian Fellowship had been at that seminar. At the same time, at the request of the minister of South Ronaldsay and Burray, the Reverend Morris Mackenzie, he had been conducting inquiries into the law concerning the uplifting of children. This followed the previous removal of eight children into care in November 1990.

With other members of the presbytery, the Reverend Brown was worried about what had taken place at the summer camp on Rousay in 1990. They were concerned about the implications of what influences were being exerted in their island society. When the police raided the manse of fellow-minister, Morris Mackenzie, in South Ronaldsay on Wednesday 27 February, their concern took on a very personal edge.

Now one of their own was implicated in alleged rituals that seemed to have sprung directly from a determined searching for satanism and rituals adopted by extremist Christian groups. Peter Brown conducted investigations and presented a report to the Orkney Presbytery.

The presbytery met in private to discuss the report, and the alleged child abuse cases in South Ronaldsay. They then issued a public statement, which was published in the March edition of *The Presbytery Bulletin*, the Orkney churches' informal news-sheet. The statement came in the form of nine motions which had been passed by the members.

First they declared their grave concern at the happenings in South Ronaldsay, and condemned the method or lack of method, used to investigate the allegations. They re-affirmed the sanctity of the family, and the rights of parents and children in the home. They regretted that there appeared to be no suitable places of safety in

Orkney if it was found to be absolutely necessary to remove children from their homes.

A decision was taken unanimously by the presbytery to support and assist the Reverend Morris Mackenzie; to share some of the burden of his parish duties, and to make life easier for him. The *Bulletin* reported that the presbytery welcomed the pastoral care already shown to the minister of South Ronaldsay and Burray and his wife, and encouraged such continuing concern.

They recognised that cases of alleged child abuse put great stress on all concerned, and they offered pastoral support to all children, parents, police, lawyers, the medical profession, social workers and anxious onlookers. The presbytery also instructed their clerk to write to the Prime Minister, John Major, the Secretary of State for Scotland, Ian Lang, the local Member of Parliament, Jim Wallace, and the Member of the European Parliament, Winnie Ewing, asking for the law concerning child abuse to be reviewed as a matter of urgency.

The clerk was also instructed to write to Orkney's Director of Social Work, Paul Lee, the Chairman of the Social Work Committee, Councillor Mrs Mairhi Trickett, and Councillor Jackie Tait, Convener of Orkney Islands Council. He was to express the presbytery's grave concern over certain aspects of the handling of these cases and press for an urgent review of procedure in suspected child abuse cases.

The presbytery asked members of the church to note that the South Ronaldsay Parents' Action Committee had set up a fund for legal aid to which they might like to contribute, and they asked their Social Matters Committee to look into the question of guidance to ministers in cases involving the Social Work Department.

They also expressed their concern that a manse and church buildings had been searched by the police, and items of an ecclesiastical nature removed. These were described as artefacts and clothing used in Christian worship and devotions, such as the broken cross, and Mr Mackenzie's funeral cloak. Professional papers had also been removed, and the Presbytery urged that a dialogue should be established between ministers of religion, police and the Social Work Department. To set this in motion, the clerk was also asked to write to the Chief Constable of the Northern Constabulary, Hugh MacMillan, and the Chief Executive of Orkney Islands Council, Ron Gilbert.

The church in Orkney had put their support squarely behind the minister and the parents in South Ronaldsay. They had also put themselves into the role of mediators, if anyone wanted to use them. There was a sadness in Orkney that religion appeared to be an element in the story. There was no proof that an initial spark from Christian extremists had set the whole affair in motion; there was suspicion, and it is one aspect of the Orkney affair that attracted the attention of the feature writers. They focused on the fact that each of the four families followed a different form of worship.

One family is, as has already been said, a Quaker family; another family belongs to the Church of Scotland, and one family is Baptist. The mother in the fourth family is Jewish, and this, said the Reverend Peter Brown, was even sadder. 'Haven't the Jews so often been the victims down the years of people who were looking for demons to bait?' he said.

Because there is no rabbi in Orkney, the Jewish family had got into the habit of worshipping with the Quakers; but the ecumenical element didn't end there. All over Orkney during the time the children were away from their homes, prayers were said for them in churches of all denominations and at prayer meetings, and despite the torment they went through, none of the parents' faiths wavered. The only message some of them had had time to give their children as the social workers took them to waiting cars was 'have faith, be strong, we'll do what we can'.

The Quaker mother, who was so astonished by the ignorance of the police when they questioned her about the way she and her family worshipped, said her faith remained strong. She had tried to describe the origins of the Quakers – or the Society of Friends – to the police, but she said they had simply found it strange. They couldn't understand the practice of mainly worshipping in silence and without a minister, or without the trappings of church rituals.

This mother said that even in the midst of all the pain and trauma of her children being taken away, she had felt surrounded and safe in the love and support of the Quaker movement. She had felt, too, the warmth and comfort coming from the general public.

In the first days she said her one hope was that her children, isolated though they were, could feel 'held' in the same safe way. If they did, then she believed they would come through all this and be reasonably all right.

The Reverend Peter Brown was worried that the police had seemed so confused about what he called 'orthodox auld kirk' Christianity, as well as the less usual religious situations such as the Quaker Movement. In an island which has an excellent record in ecumenicism, a seeming lack of understanding and intolerance was a great source of concern. A former chaplain in the Royal Navy, Peter Brown has lived amongst and mixed with people of many creeds and cultures. He practises what he has always preached – respect and tolerance for people of whatever religion, who try to live a good life by their own creed. He continued his investigation and on 12 April 1991 presented a very full report to the Islands' Presbytery.

During the 1980s, when allegations of satanic ritual abuse multiplied, as has been stated, not one single case was backed by any forensic evidence, either in Britain or in the United States. In some cases, the lack of forensic evidence had actually disproved the allegations and exposed the witnesses as perjurors. Yet new waves of allegations continued. They were rejected in Rochdale, and even in Nottingham, where cases of sexual abuse were upheld, and nine parents were found to have been involved in elaborate and organised abuse, there was no evidence that they did this as part of any satanic rituals or worship.

In Orkney, the idea of devil worship was seen as ridiculous. The neighbours of the four involved families were vehement that there was nothing like this going on. Anger began to grow, fuelled by the possibility that because certain extremists seemed to go out of their way to look for signs of Satan in every aspect of everyday life, people living quiet, caring family lives had been put into a state of terror and agony.

Experts in the field are questioning the basis on which the satanic abuse war is being fought. They say that social workers who attend seminars and lectures on the subject do not realise that these ideas are being promoted by Christian Fundamentalist extremists who believe that all abuse is demonic in origin.

Social workers, who are justifiably worried about the growth of abuse, are eager to catch hold of new ideas, but they have failed repeatedly to realise that they are not being given proof. They are being told to go out and search for it. Applying the satanic indicators, they can find signs anywhere, but they have never been able to furnish proof. The public remains sceptical, but those who support the notion of satanic abuse say that social workers must not fall into the trap of believing it does not exist, just because it is difficult to prove. That is all the more reason, they believe, for keeping their crusade going, so that a wider public will react positively and begin to recognise the indicators of abuse.

On 4 April 1991, the very day the children were finally flown home to Orkney, the government announced it had commissioned an Inquiry to establish the extent – if any – of ritual sexual abuse of children. The announcement came from the Department of Health, besieged by a welter of conflicting evidence. They said the inquiry would be headed by Professor Jean La Fontaine, Professor of Social Anthropology at the London School of Economics. Her remit would be to talk to social services departments, the police and the Home Office; she would examine documents on all reported cases of ritual abuse, and draw up her report within two years.

A Home Office spokesman was quoted as saying: 'The object is to investigate whether children are being abused in an organised way by networks or rings of adults. Such organised abuse may be satanic or ritual, but we do not use those terms. Everyone in the world seems to have a view on this subject, but no one knows whether it exists or not.'

CHAPTER EIGHT

Processes of Law

Events in Orkney seemed to gather their own momentum. Hearings and appeals became part of the pattern of life for the families, their legal advisers, their friends and supporters, and indeed for the press and media corps that were reporting what was happening to the outside world.

A report on the case involving the removal of the nine South Ronaldsay children from their homes was sent by the police to the Procurator Fiscal in Wick. At that time Orkney did not have its own full-time Procurator Fiscal. The office was shared with Wick. The situation has been altered since, and although Orkney still does not have its own Procurator Fiscal, it now shares one with Shetland. It is maintained that neither group of islands will lose out from this arrangement, even in emergencies, as there are deputies in both Kirkwall and Lerwick who can act on police reports.

The Northern Constabulary carried out independent enquiries into the case. Quite separately from the Social Work Department in Orkney, they investigated the information that led to the uplifting of the children. The police reached the same conclusions, agreeing that the nine children were severely at risk, and they cooperated in the early morning raids.

Part of the police investigations involved a young policewoman from the Northern Constabulary. Linda Williamson worked with the RSSPCC social worker, Liz McLean in most of the interviews with the eight children from Orkney's large problem family, who had been taken into care in November 1990. These interviews included the unrecorded but crucial 'disclosures' with three of them.

Police evidence was sent to the Procurator Fiscal, who had to decide whether there were grounds enough for criminal prosecutions to proceed. He put the matter into the hands of the Crown Office for a decision from a higher authority than his own. The Lord Advocate ordered further enquiries to be made.

This move was interpreted in two ways. Firstly, it could be argued that there was not sufficient evidence to warrant a criminal prosecution, and the Crown Office would need more if this was to proceed; and secondly, that there was enough evidence to make it impossible to drop the case, but more was needed to make it substantial.

Police enquiries in Orkney continued. On Wednesday 20 March, three weeks after the dawn raids, Mr and Mrs H, the fourth family whose children had been removed, were suddenly taken to Kirkwall Police Station for questioning. These were the parents who had not been questioned, nor had their house been searched on the morning of 27 February. They had however, been subject to the same grounds for referral and allegations as the other three families at the first Children's Panel Hearing on 5 March.

This was the family where the father was a semi-invalid. His health had already suffered considerably since the removal of his children, and his condition had deteriorated. The hours undergoing questioning at the police headquarters were an added strain; but it had been an extra strain, too, waiting to be questioned, and not knowing when or if it would happen.

Police activity increased. The suspects were kept under surveillance. The beleaguered families reported that their homes were being watched. Cars sat at the ends of roads for hours. The occupants were observing whoever came and went. Some parents even said they had been aware of being watched for some considerable time.

This was March – it was cold, windy, and altogether an unpleasant time of the year to have to sit in a car for long periods observing people's activities, and how they lived their lives. One of the mothers said she felt quite sorry for the police officers involved and was tempted to offer them warm drinks to keep out the cold!

On the same day as the H parents were questioned, the interim Reporter to Orkney's Children's Panel, Gordon Sloan, petitioned the Court of Session in Edinburgh. He asked their Lordships for the forthcoming Proof before the Sheriff to be heard away from Orkney in mainland Scotland. His request caused even more anger amongst the families and their supporters.

In his petition, the Reporter claimed the move to the mainland would be in the best interests of the children. He said it would be traumatic for them to be flown home to Orkney for the Proof Hearing, only to be flown away again afterwards.

The Court of Session, the highest court in Scotland, convened on Tuesday 26 March. It was led by the Lord President, Lord Hope,

sitting with Lords Mayfield and Murray, three of Scotland's most
senior judges. Before the Bench, Mr Sloan's Counsel, Lynda Clarke,
QC, made the request for the move away from Orkney. She referred
to previous Panel Hearings and Court Appeals in Kirkwall having
been 'mobbed' by demonstrators. A spokesman for the parents, when
Lynda Clarke's submission was heard, was quick to contradict this
statement, saying the supporters outside both the Panel offices and
the Sheriff Court had been orderly and quiet. The Reverend Derek
Edwards, Vice-Chairman of the Action Committee, described all the
demonstrations as 'warm and supportive'. He said the atmosphere at
each gathering had been one of calm, loving concern, and this would
continue for as long as it took to get the children home.

Mr Sloan's QC also maintained that the 'fairly horrific publicity'
and local hostility in Orkney might not only affect the children. If
the Proof was heard in Kirkwall she said it would be prejudicial to
certain adult witnesses that would be called. These witnesses would
include social workers, teachers, police officers and psychologists.

The other side of the picture was the very severe hardship that
would be faced by the families, their witnesses and supporters if they
all had to travel out of Orkney for the case. Many were involved in
farming, which at that time of the year meant that cows were calving,
ewes beginning to have their lambs, and people were generally busy
in the spring-time agricultural work. Their farms could not be left
unattended at this crucial time.

If the parents and their witnesses had to travel to the Scottish
mainland, this would involve them not only in time away they
couldn't spare, but also travelling and accommodation expenses.
There would also be the difficulty of finding people to look after
the farms while they were away. The Parents' Action Committee
was outspoken in its condemnation of this possibility. Such a move
would, they said, impose severe hardship and very great practical
problems at a time when the families had more than enough distress
to cope with. The parents' lawyers made the same points. The
parents' interests, they said, had to be considered as well as the
children's.

Committee Chairman Helen Martini, however, said that if any
such decision was *really* in the best interests of the children, they
would happily go along with it. They all wanted whatever was
best for the nine children they all missed so much. She promised
the community's support and help if indeed the parents and their

witnesses had to leave the island. No matter how long it took, she said, those who were left in South Ronaldsay would work out shifts on the various farms. The calving and lambing would be taken care of somehow.

The Court of Session, with the wisdom of Solomon, decided that the Proof Hearing should be split. The children's evidence would be heard in the Sheriff's Chambers in Inverness, and the rest of the case taken in Kirkwall Sheriff Court. Giving their decision, Lord Hope said strong reasons had been given for hearing what the children had to say without taking them back to Orkney. It might indeed be contrary to their best interests to travel back to their island home. He said, however, that the court could see no reason for the Reporter's adult witnesses having to be heard away from Kirkwall.

The three senior judges agreed that a balance had to be struck between the interests of the children and their parents – and Lord Hope said the parents' interests were also of very great importance. He stressed that attempts should be made to minimise any hardship they might experience to the greatest extent possible, as long as these did not prejudice the children's best interests. Lord Hope also asked the Scottish Legal Aid Board to act urgently to lessen any hardship to the parents.

The decision of the three judges satisfied most of the parties concerned. The parents and their support group were pleased. Committee Chairman, Helen Martini, said it was a very sensible, if unusual decision. No one wanted the children to be more traumatised than they already were, she said, and it would certainly be less travelling for them to go to Inverness than to return to Kirkwall.

The children's Curators – the lawyers appointed by the court to look solely after the children's interests – had also been in favour of the children being heard in Inverness. Taking them back to Orkney, they felt, would have deprived them of the privacy they needed. The Curators, with no other concerns in the matter, were truly speaking in the best interests of the children.

Parents' Committee Vice-Chairman, Derek Edwards, described the decision as a 'working compromise'. The parents had to be able to present a full defence, he said, and if the whole case had been heard in Inverness, it would have been almost impossible to fully safeguard their interests and get everybody in the right place at the right time. Mr Edwards was delighted that for the very first time someone had started to consider the interests of the parents. He urged everyone concerned to take note of what the Lord President had said.

The Court of Session decision was taken on Tuesday 26 March – just one day after the twenty-one day Place of Safety Orders on the nine children had expired. A further Hearing of Orkney Children's Panel had been held on 25 March to extend the orders and keep the children in care. Again supporters and the press gathered outside the terraced house in Kirkwall that serves as Orkney's Children's Panel Offices. Again the four families, accompanied by their representatives, went inside. Again the nine children were absent, and the Place of Safety orders were extended for a further twenty-one days. One difference this time was that each of the parents was accompanied by either a senior or a junior Counsel. These people were to be their 'lay' representatives, as, of course, the Panel Hearings are not Courts of Law, and lawyers as such have no role there.

One of the great strengths of the Hearing system in Scotland is its informality. The lay panel, the rights of parents and children to be accompanied by a friend or supporter, and the complete absence of any professional legal formality generally help to reduce the tension and create a situation for discussion. The presence of the high-powered lawyers at this second Children's Hearing in Orkney immediately charged the atmosphere.

The Hearing began with a formal decision to dispense with the presence of the children. The Reporter, Gordon Sloan, told the three Panel Members that the grounds for referral had not changed since the last Hearing three weeks previously. He considered it was potentially damaging to the children to be at the Hearing, and, besides, the case of Proof before the Sheriff was still pending. The Panel agreed it would have been too traumatic for the children to bring them back. The Chairman, Mrs Jean Robertson, said the risk of the children meeting their parents and other local people was too great, given the serious nature of the allegations. And so the presence of the nine children was quickly dispensed with. They were not to have the grounds of referral explained to them, or a chance to have their say, for the second time.

The lawyers acting for the parents tried to present themselves as friends, representatives who would speak on behalf of the parents. This was not easy, and they unavoidably sounded like lawyers arguing a case. Gordon Sloan, the Interim Reporter, took great exception to their presence. He threatened repeatedly to have them removed from the Hearing for disrupting the proceedings. At one stage he threatened to remove solicitor John Moir from the room, too. He accused Mr Moir of 'sniggering'. In making these threats, Mr Sloan exceeded his authority. The role of the Reporter is to advise the Panel, and keep the proceedings within the framework of the law. It is *not* to dictate the course of the Hearing, and only the Chairman of the Panel can have a person removed. Mr Sloan, however, appeared to adopt an attitude of being 'in charge'. One of the parents accused him of 'smiling when it was completely inappropriate to do so'.

The Panel Chairman told the parents that their children were well, settling down in their foster homes, and that some were going to school. One child was being tutored at home, and they were all fine. One mother, Mrs B, was very distressed when she heard this.

'It's just like hospital patter,' she said. 'It tells me nothing about my children, and I shouldn't have to keep contacting the Social Work Department to find out how they are. They should contact me.'

She was told that two of her three children were together in one foster home, but was given no information as to where in Scotland they were. She was told one of her daughters was receiving tuition in her foster home. This was later found to be untrue, as neither of her daughters nor her son received any schooling or tuition of any sort for the five weeks they were away. She complained that her children had apparently not been allowed access to a Baptist minister, but was told that they had not asked for religious support when it was offered.

The advocate acting as her representative said she believed matters had changed very substantially since the last hearing. It was now known that the allegations had come from statements made from three children already in care in mainland Scotland. These three, also from South Ronaldsay, had been abused, and were undergoing extensive questioning about it. It was known, too, she said, that medical examinations on the nine children in the present case, had revealed no signs of abuse. She told the Panel that the original allegations could not be taken at face value, and that children shouldn't be taken into care on the unchecked allegations of other children.

Mr Sloan constantly interrupted. The line she was taking was not proper for a Hearing, he said. This was *not* a Court of Law. The only concern for the Panel was whether the children had to be in compulsory care.

Questions were also asked about what guidelines the Social Work Department had or had not used. The Reporter said this was not a concern of the Children's Panel. They were straying back into the realms of evidence, and that would be a matter for the court when the Proof was heard.

The proceedings for the four families followed much the same pattern. In each case their representative raised the question of the lack of medical evidence, and said the authorities should not have rushed to take children into care on the basis of unchecked statements from other children. Several times the Reporter interrupted and threatened to remove them.

All the parents were told that their children were in very nice foster homes, with very nice families. In one case this turned out to be quite untrue. A fifteen-year-old boy, the oldest of the nine, had been taken to a secure unit. Geilsland School is a residential establishment in Beith, run by the Church of Scotland in Ayrshire. It's the sort of establishment formerly called a List D school, a place for youngsters who have, for example, committed offences or were beyond parental control. This boy had never been in trouble with the law in his life. His parents, furthermore, had requested that he and his eleven-year-old brother should be placed in a Quaker boarding school. One such school had immediately offered places and declared that it would abide by any access restrictions laid upon it. But this school was not considered by the authorities to be a suitable place of safety. They told these parents that it was preferable, anyway, for the boy to have the comfort and security of a good foster home. The parents didn't know then that a List D school was considered suitable for their son. More of that, however, later.

The Reporter's request to the Children's Panel for an extension of the Place of Safety orders for a further twenty-one days was upheld. The children were to remain where they were – wherever that was the parents were to remain in ignorance, with the children still isolated.

The parents' impassioned pleas that the best places of safety for their children were with their families was disregarded. Mrs B asked that her children be sent to their father, who was working in England, and had not been implicated in the allegations of abuse. That, too, was disregarded. The agony of not knowing where, or how their children were, continued. The parents' pain on behalf of their children was almost too much to bear. They believed their children were being abused by the system set up to protect them.

Derek Edwards, speaking after the Place of Safety orders were extended, said that although they had all more or less expected this to happen, it was another blow for the parents. They had come out of the Hearing without their children, and without knowing how long it might be before they were able to be together again. He said that although the public faces of the parents were brave, and they were trying to bear up, there were times when they sank to the depths of despair. They all knew that they had to go on fighting, and be strong for their children, and Mr Edwards commended them for that strength.

He repeated that the Action Committee should call for change. It was a cry that was gathering support all over the country. The laws concerning child care and child protection had to be reviewed and changed for the benefit of all children. It was absolutely essential that everyone in every position of authority in child-care organisations, local authorities and government should take this on board, he said. He also called for a full investigation into Orkney's Social Work Department, and the RSSPCC whose involvement was turning out to be very much more fundamental than had at first been supposed.

The lawyers, working away in their legal centre in Kirkwall, continued to prepare their case for the Proof Hearing, which was due to open in Kirkwall on 3 April. This was now only a week away. There was still a great deal of work to be done. Other distractions kept cropping up to delay their work, however – like the publication in a Scottish Sunday newspaper of an alleged statement from Orkney Islands Council Temporary Press Officer, Nick Clayton. The story quoted him as saying there was medical evidence which showed that there had been abuse. It was the main lead story and was written by one of the paper's most respected journalists.

News of its intended publication filtered through to Orkney late on the Saturday night. The parents, their lawyers and supporters, as well as the Islands Council and their own legal advisers, were aghast and very angry. The parents' lawyers, acting through an Edinburgh firm, tried late that night to get an interim interdict to stop publication. Orkney Islands Council, too, tried to prevent the story appearing in the following day's edition.

Lord Penrose, hearing the interdict late at night in his home, turned it down. It was too late by this time to stop the presses rolling, and the first editions had already been despatched. He said there had been sufficient time to bring an action, and awarded costs against the parents. There was great anger in the parents' support group. Helen Martini said if this was evidence that had been leaked, it would be very prejudicial to the Proof Hearing due to begin the following week. If the Council's Temporary Press Officer, who had been appointed solely to deal with the alleged child abuse controversy, had been given such confidential information, she said, they wanted to know who had given it to him. She found it hard to believe that a Press Officer would be party to evidence of this nature. This was a police matter, and such information should only be divulged to the legal teams, and possibly to the families, she said. It was certainly not for general release to the public.

The Chief Executive of Orkney Islands Council, Ron Gilbert, was furious too. The council had heard about impending publication late on Saturday night, too, he said, and had tried to stop it by taking out an interdict against the newspaper concerned. Mr Gilbert stated categorically that only very few council officials would be party to such information, and would certainly not release it. Nor would they, he said, under any circumstances, give it to the Press Officer. Mr Clayton had not had this evidence, and nor, claimed the Chief Executive, had he said so to the journalists. He was appalled that such a story should appear in a newspaper, and the council, he said, would meet to determine what should be done about it.

It was expected that some sort of legal action would follow. A press statement was issued by Ron Gilbert on behalf of the council, emphatically denying that medical evidence of alleged child abuse had been 'leaked' to a Sunday newspaper. The statement continued: 'A journalist was given a briefing by the council's acting Press Officer, Nick Clayton, on the general Scottish Office guidelines for dealing with child sexual abuse . . . . During this briefing Mr Clayton said nothing about what medical evidence may exist relating to the nine children subject to Place of Safety warrants. Since his recent appointment Mr Clayton has at no time had access to any medical evidence relating to the nine children. He has not been informed as to terms of any such evidence by officials of Orkney Islands Council's Social Work Department . . . It is specifically denied that during the briefing Mr Clayton stated that in relation to the nine children there exists medical evidence "consistent with some form of abuse" which has been found during examinations carried out by a police surgeon.'

No action was taken against the newspaper, however, and one journalist, who had taken legal advice himself over the story, steadfastly maintained that he had quoted Nick Clayton's comments completely accurately.

With this unwelcome interruption behind them, Alistair Bruce and John Moir continued, with the QCs and advocates, to prepare their case for the Proof Hearing. It was a preparation time fraught with difficulties and frustrations. The Reporter, Gordon Sloan, was unhelpful. They said he was unwilling to show them the evidence he had been given so they could adequately prepare their case for the parents. It is normal procedure for this sort of evidence to be made available to defence lawyers, although in a civil case it is not a legal requirement. Finally the lawyers for the families went to court again to try to obtain sight of at least some of the evidence against their clients.

They spent Thursday 28 March presenting 'Minutes and Motions' before Sheriff David Kelbie in Kirkwall Sheriff Court. They wanted him to direct Mr Sloan to release the evidence against the parents, and at the end of the day they were only partially successful.

The two solicitors had been very busy dashing round Orkney gathering character witnesses. They had taken the very unusual step of advertising in the local newspaper for anyone to come forward who knew of any ritual practices that might have been taking place in South Ronaldsay. They were not at all surprised when they didn't receive a single reply. They were overwhelmed with replies, however, when they asked if people were prepared to come forward as character-witnesses for the parents of the nine South Ronaldsay children whose plight had moved the nation. They set up sessions where people could come and talk about the families, and make statements about the sort of people they were. In just a few days over eighty people came forward, eager to support, and to add their voices and their knowledge of their neighbours to the case. The two Kirkwall solicitors worked day and night to gather and collate these statements. They were overwhelmed by the response, and by the willingness of so many to step forward and be counted in court when the time came.

These witnesses were the main thrust of the defence for the parents. 'Innocent until proven guilty' does not apply in cases such as these. All that has to be established is that 'on the balance of probabilities' the alleged offence took place. The parents felt that the normal protection of the law had been reversed and they had to prove their innocence, rather than the law having to prove their guilt. They were up against the absolute certainty of guilt expressed by all the parties weighed against them. Orkney's Social Work Department, whose leading officials apparently had no doubt at all that the parents were all guilty of abusing their children. This view was evidently shared by other bodies involved in the case, and one particular representative of the RSSPCC, Raymond Starr, when asked if they were really sure of their ground and that the children had had to be removed from their homes in the devastating dawn raid, had replied: 'Oh yes. If you knew what we know, you'd realise we had to take the action we did.'

But proof positive they did not have to supply. A decision is made only on the balance of probabilities. This means a case does not have to be proved beyond all reasonable doubt. If there is enough to suggest that it is more probable that the offence took place, that is enough for the action that was taken by all the agencies involved in Orkney.

CHAPTER NINE

Social Workers: Friends or Enemies?

Orkney Islands Council's Social Work Department is a small one. In recent years the Department has been starved of financial resources which has led to many of the serious problems faced by succeeding directors. Within a ten year period the department has also been the subject of two investigations by the Social Work Services Group, the social work arm of the Scottish Office.

In 1981 concerns over the way the Social Work Department operated led to an inquiry, the results of which have never been made public. At around the same time, Orkney Islands Council officials made their first attempt to remove the Reporter to Orkney's Children's Panel, Mrs Katherine Kemp, from office. Then, as in 1991, they were unsuccessful. She continued to work as Reporter for the Islands until she was locked out of her office and suspended by the Chief Executive in March 1990.

During the 1980s problems beset Orkney's Social Work Department. Questions were asked about the way in which Camoran, the children's home in Kirkwall, was run. There were allegations that things there were not right. The small department, short of manpower and finance, was stretched to the limit, and worse was to come. The then Director of Social Work, Hugh MacGillivray, was asked to drastically cut back his department's budget.

This was at a time when the work load was growing. As in many areas, an increasingly ageing population was becoming an added drain on scant resources. At the same time child abuse, following a national pattern, was becoming more widely acknowledged and symptoms recognised. This was not a time to cut back the resources of the department which deals with the most acute form of social need, but a time to expand, provide more personnel, more finance, and more expertise.

In October/November 1989, Orkney's Social Work Department was the subject of another Social Work Services Group investigation. Two social workers asked for this to be done, because they were so concerned about the policy they were supposed to be implementing.

The report was completed, and sent to the senior officials of the council. It is believed to have been highly critical of the way the department was operating, but again the contents of that report have never been disclosed.

The elected members of Orkney Islands Council were each handed a copy of that report at a meeting of the council. They were allowed to see it for one hour, before it was taken back, and none of them has been able to get hold of it since. Several have tried. Councillor Ian MacDonald and former Councillor Spencer Rosie made a number of requests to officials for copies of the document. They were unsuccessful. Even the Member of Parliament, Jim Wallace, has been unable to obtain a copy of what is thought to be a damning indictment of Orkney Islands Council Social Work Department.

Hugh MacGillivray, the beleaguered Director of Social Work, handed in his resignation. Some of the social workers followed suit. The way was set for much-needed change, but would things change for the better?

The man appointed by Orkney Islands Council to succeed Mr MacGillivray was a Yorkshireman, Paul Lee. With his photograph in every newspaper in the country, and regular shots of him on television during much of 1991, Mr Lee has become well known, by sight at least. He came into the department in Orkney at a time of crisis, his remit to operate on a shoestring budget, and to repair social work's damaged reputation. Many people in Orkney believed he was succeeding – until the morning of 27 February 1991.

Although it later transpired that the RSSPCC were contracted by the Social Work Department to remove and question the South Ronaldsay children, at the time it was generally understood that Orkney's own social workers were mainly involved. Paul Lee immediately became a man under siege. A quiet, reserved, almost taciturn man, he was ill-equipped to cope with the bombardment of questions from the press and media reporters. He retreated into monosyllabic replies, giving no clues as to the origins of the information that led to the removal of nine children. He stuck rigidly to his statement that what had been done was absolutely essential in the best interests of the children.

The few brief interviews he gave to journalists were terse, and could be described as defensive. He said people would have had cause to criticise if his department had failed to act following the information they had received. He repeated, together with the

Chairman of the Social Work Committee, Mrs Mairhi Trickett, that seven o'clock in the morning was the right time to take the children, as it was a time when families would all be together. That early hour also avoided having to go to the schools to take children, an action which had caused such controversy in November 1990. Mr Lee stood firmly by the decisions that had been taken in collaboration with members of the RSSPCC, who had been involved from the beginning in the disclosure work with the eight W children who'd been taken away then.

Mr Lee, who came to Orkney after ten years working in Scotland, in both Highland and Grampian Regions, was reluctant to talk to the media. One press conference was held in the week following the children's removal; during it Mr Lee denied emphatically that there was any sort of a vendetta taking place. Feelings were being expressed freely in some quarters that the whole matter had been one of 'revenge' for support shown to the W family after eight children from the family of fifteen had been taken away three months before. This was certainly not the case, Mr Lee said.

'We were acting jointly with the police,' he said, 'having received information which pertained to potential offences against children'.

At that time Paul Lee did not rule out the possibility of other families in South Ronaldsay being involved in the ritual sexual abuse that was alleged. He said that his department was concentrating its activities on the investigation in hand, for the time being. There was an implication, however, that more was to come.

That 'concentration' on the current investigation involved a senior social worker, Sue Millar, working as Team Leader. She liaised with the RSSPCC social workers on the mainland who were dealing with the children, and conducted meetings in Orkney about the case. She did not, however, conduct any multi-disciplinary case conferences about the children until after they had been returned to their homes. She did not consult with the children's family doctors, or their class teachers at school. She was described by parents and Action Committee members as a hard woman, with no emotion, no compassion. She did nothing to help the stricken families, to advise, or to offer information on either the Social Work Department's rights and responsibilities, or those of the parents. Her responses to all questions by the parents were criticised by them as 'text-book jargon'. She used the same lines over and over again, wearing a fixed smile on her face. A smile, the parents said, which was devoid of any emotion.

They all felt her attitude was hostile and aggressive, throughout the weeks that followed the removal of their children and after their return home. In June 1991 Sue Millar left Orkney's Social Work Department saying this move, to further another strand in her career, had been planned at the beginning of the year.

Condemnation of the way in which the Social Work Department had handled the case came from all sides. The South Ronaldsay Parents Action Committee wrote in protest to the Secretary of State, Ian Lang. Orkney Presbytery followed suit, stating their very grave misgivings about the procedures followed by Orkney Islands Council. The lawyers reiterated their concern about the legality of the actions taken.

Calls from every side for a full judicial inquiry into the whole affair grew louder. MP Jim Wallace made his appeal for such an inquiry on the floor of the House of Commons; and when the topic was brought up at the Scottish Liberal Democrats Conference, he was supported by Judy Steel, wife of the former leader of the Liberal Party, and herself one of the first ever Reporters to a Children's Panel when the system began in 1971. Several of Orkney's councillors, too, began to support the call for an inquiry.

All the political parties spoke of their concern in one way or another. Each of the prospective parliamentary candidates for Orkney and Shetland added their voices to the growing storm of unrest. Labour's John Aberdein talked to colleagues at the Scottish Labour Party Conference; the Conservative candidate, Hampshire barrister Dr Paul McCormick, made an immediate and thorough study of the circumstances surrounding the removal of the children, and Frances McKie for the Scottish National Party was quick to express her horror of the Social Work Department's actions. A teacher, employed by Orkney Islands Council, she said there was an atmosphere of great insecurity amongst council employees about there right to protest at that time. She herself received what she termed 'strong advice' not to get involved.

The Scottish National Party Euro-MP for the Highlands and Islands, Winnie Ewing, wrote to the Secretary of State for Scotland, detailing some of the correspondence she had received from worried parents. She said it was a clear infringement of human rights to deny parents access to their children. Following her enquiries in South Ronaldsay, she said it was clear that the law was not complied with at all times, and that grave irregularities had occurred. There could well be, she continued, a case for the Court of Human Rights in Strasbourg.

It was no wonder that the Social Work Department in general, and Paul Lee in particular, felt under siege. There was no doubt, however, that Mr Lee could have made the situation a little easier for himself, and his staff, if he had been a bit more open with the press. His very short statements, and constant insistence that they had done the right thing, made it difficult, if not impossible, to reflect the point of the view of 'the other side' – the side of the authorities, who then complained that the parents had too much publicity and had the full support of the press and media. Comments like 'if I was one of those parents, I'd be so ashamed I'd want to keep out of the limelight' were heard from some of those connected with the local authority.

It is true that the families, because of their own determination and because the course of events dictated the coverage, got the lion's share of the publicity. The press began to be accused of being one-sided, unfair, of not giving a balanced picture. At that time, there was no sight of the other half of the picture, and until Orkney Islands Council appointed a temporary Press Officer, no regular statements were made.

The council's temporary Press Officer, Nick Clayton, did not appear to help their cause very much. He would only read out short prepared statements, and would neither comment on them, nor give journalists any access to the people who could. Ranks were closed. Mr Clayton was simply a front man. He fielded the phone calls and promised answers – answers which never came. Frustration grew. The Parents' Action Committee wrote to Orkney Islands Council asking who was supplying Nick Clayton with the information he was giving to the press. They wanted to know urgently, they said, who decided to employ him, and who checked his credentials. At times, especially following the leakage of so-called 'medical evidence' to a Sunday newspaper, it appeared he was acting independently.

The frustration turned to anger on more than one occasion. News that the Islands' social workers had been given professional stress therapy astounded the families and their support organisation. The Secretary of the British Association of Social Workers, Dennis Gower, confirmed that experienced case workers had visited Orkney to support five social workers involved in the South Ronaldsay case. He said they were under 'some considerable stress'. Although social workers were trained in dealing with stress, said Mr Gower, the whole subject of removing children from their parents was no less emotive for them than for other members of the community.

Dr Helen Martini, Chairman of the Action Committee, was almost speechless with anger. How dare the council obtain stress counselling for the social workers, she asked, when the agonised parents of the nine children were under the sort of stress the social workers couldn't even begin to imagine? She described their action as callous and insensitive. The parents hadn't been offered any sort of advice or counselling; they had all received a letter from Paul Lee inviting them to come and talk to his department, but no one had offered them any information about their children; if they wanted that they had to ring up the department and ask for it. No one had asked how they were coping, or attempted to offer at the very least a listening ear.

Dennis Gower said that the press coverage of the events in Orkney had been mainly anti-social work because they were unable to answer back. The parents and their action group had been free to talk to the press. The social workers were bound by rules of confidentiality and legal requirements which prevented them from revealing any relevant information.

Mary Hartnoll, Director of Social Work in Grampian Region, and Secretary of the Association of Social Work Directors, entered the debate. She said that there was a great deal of strain on all concerned, the children, the families and the social workers, wherever there were child abuse allegations. What made it more difficult for the social workers in Orkney, she said, was the very small size of the department; they had few colleagues with whom to share the stress.

Following as it did the enormous publicity that surrounded the child abuse allegations in Cleveland, Nottingham, and Rochdale, Orkney Islands Council were strangely unprepared for the wide interest their own case attracted. This was the first time a Social Work Department in Scotland had come under such public fire for the same reasons.

It was not, however, the first time that questions had been asked about Social Work Departments in Scotland. Departments in Fife, Aberdeen, Strathclyde, Shetland and Dumfries and Galloway have all been subject to criticism and controversy regarding their handling of child care and protection during and since the late 1980s. The question that continues to haunt many people, both

The normal peace and tranquillity of South Ronaldsay.
Photograph © Robert Black

Where it all began. The village of St Margaret's Hope in South
Ronaldsay, where two of the families live, and all the younger children
go to school. *Photograph* © Sharyn Crossley

The last of four man-made causeways known as the Churchill Barriers
linking Orkney's mainland to its scattered and remote south isles.
Photograph © Robert Black

The quarry on South Ronaldsay where the alleged abuse was supposed
to have taken place. *Photograph* © Robert Black

The Reverend Morris Mackenzie, Church of Scotland minister of South Ronaldsay and Burray. *Photograph* © Orkney Photographic

Family solicitor John Moir talking to the media after a hearing of
Orkney Children's Panel confirmed Place of Safety orders on the nine
children. *Photograph* © Orkney Photographic

Orcadians and incomers join together in a peaceful demonstration outside
the Children's Panel office in Kirkwall as a hearing takes place.
Photograph © Sharyn Crossley

The solicitors and representatives of the South Ronaldsay Parents' Action Committee hold a press conference in a Kirkwall night club. Pictured left to right: Alistair Bruce, John Moir, Dr Helen Martini, the Reverend Derek Edwards. *Photograph* © Sharyn Crossley

Paul Lee, director of Orkney Social Work Department, and Social Work Committee chairman Mrs Mairhi Trickett, facing the press to explain their action in removing the children. *Photograph* © Sharyn Crossley

Former reporter to Orkney Children's Panel, Mrs Katherine Kemp.
Photograph © Orkney Photographic

Gordon Sloan, acting interim reporter to Orkney Children's Panel.
Photograph © Orkney Photographic

Sheriff David Kelbie. *Photograph* © Orkney Photographic

Lord Clyde, appointed by the Secretary of State to lead the Inquiry,
outside Kirkwall Town Hall. *Photograph* © Sharyn Crossley

Dr Helen Martini, chairman of South Ronaldsay Parents' Action
Committee, after hearing the children are coming home.
Photograph © Orkney Photographic

Friends and well-wishers gather at Kirkwall Airport to await the return
of the children to Orkney. *Photograph* © Sharyn Crossley

inside and outside of the social work profession, is just how deep is the problem?

No one doubts the huge work-loads that these departments face. The amount of child protection work has increased massively in recent years. More cases of abuse are coming to light, and children have to be protected; some children have to be rescued from the living hell they have to endure. There has to be a force which operates truly in the best interests of the child, and there has to be recognition and understanding of the very difficult and narrow lines many social workers have to tread in dealing with the most harrowing cases. They have to have public support or their jobs would be untenable, but perhaps they also need to be less rigid and more approachable.

Social workers should never have to be in a situation where a small child slips through the net and dies. That sort of episode makes them subject to public outrage. The feelings of outrage are the same as when large numbers of children are taken from their homes simultaneously on unsubstantiated allegations of child abuse. The outrage reaches epic proportions when people realise that no cross-checking has been done, no enquiries made from the people who have regular dealings with the children.

The question must then be asked: who protects the children from the protectors? Who is there to put the brakes on these outbreaks of zeal, and the absolute belief that, no matter how bizarre, the allegations are water-tight?

In June 1991, following the trauma in Orkney, the government announced categorically that no more children were to be taken from their homes by social workers in dawn raids. The only exception would be if a child's life was in danger. This became law immediately in England and Wales, and is part of the new Children's Act. It was believed that similar action would follow very quickly in Scotland, where the Child Care Law Review was nearing completion. This review of child-care in Scotland began before the children in Orkney were taken from their homes early on a February morning. Its completion was delayed because of the case.

In reviewing child-care law, the Scottish Office took submissions from every agency involved with the care, protection and management of children. These included Social Work Departments, children's homes, Children's Hearing Panels, voluntary organisations, and others. Many proposals have been made to tighten the law and offer real care and protection to children, the most vulnerable members of society. In the light of the inquiry into the Orkney affair, it is likely that these submissions will have to be looked at again, and new laws drafted.

Meanwhile, the relationship between the Social Work Department and the families and their representatives was not an easy one. The families were pressing for information, for assurances; the department was, if not directly hostile, certainly defensive, according to the parents and the Action Committee which supported them. Communication between them was at a minimum.

Communications sent to the children in care, however, blossomed. The Social Work Department duly acknowledged the receipt of letters sent to the nine children care of the department. The Parents' Action Committee was sent lists of letters the department claimed to have forwarded to the children, with each addressee mentioned by name. In the early days, individuals who sent letters received a standard reply from Paul Lee.

This reply read: 'I duly acknowledge receipt of correspondence sent in respect of children in care and confirm that the mail has now been forwarded accordingly.'

One Aberdeen correspondent, who received this, and who later realised that the children hadn't received the letters she had sent them, felt very aggrieved. She wrote to the Director of Social Work and accused him of lying.

Paul Lee replied: 'Thank you for your letter of 2 May 1991. All mail received in respect of the children to whom you refer was sent by this office to workers involved directly with the children. If mail did not reach them by the time of their discharge from care, it was not intentional. All mail, which was subsequently returned to this office, has been passed to the families concerned. I am sorry if you feel aggrieved. There was no intention to misinform you about the situation.' In fact this correspondent initially wrote to the children soon after they were taken to mainland Scotland.

One writer, who enclosed stamps for forwarding his letter to the children, had these returned to him, with a letter from Paul Lee to say the mail had been duly forwarded, and that the council had its own forwarding system, so he was returning the stamps.

It is known that none of the three thousand or so of letters were received by the children until their return home. The first batch arrived the day they went home. These had been written weeks before. Indeed, some that are known to have been sent have never been returned.

The deluge of letters that continued to arrive in the Social Work Department eventually made personal replies an impossible task for the Department. Their right to withhold correspondence from the children in care must, however, be questioned. These nine children were allowed no crumbs of comfort whatsoever. Not even the knowledge that hundreds of people, friends and strangers, cared about their plight, and wanted simply to say so. The hand of friendship, extended so warmly by so many, was rudely brushed aside by those who believed they knew best. It was, they considered, all in the best interests of the children.

The South Ronaldsay Parents' Action Committee wrote to the Islands Council repeatedly. They asked for a delegation to meet the Social Work Committee; they asked the Director of Social Work to meet with the Action Committee Chairman and Vice-Chairman to discuss the report issued by the organisation PAIN. They also wanted to talk about Mr Lee's policy for dealing with the action group, and asked that a meeting should take place as quickly as possible; no replies were received to these letters, and the requests were made repeatedly.

Eventually a reply came from the Islands' Director of Administration and Legal Services, Rowan McCallum. He stated that, because matters relating to the issue in question were sub judice, it would be very difficult to meet with the Parents' Committee. Mr McCallum continued that the decisions made by the Social Work Department were made on the basis of confidential information, and should that department reply to the Action Committee, he said, they might divulge information which should not be revealed at that time.

He did, however, acknowledge that it would be neither responsible nor sensible to ignore the existence of the Action Committee, and he offered them the opportunity of a meeting with representatives of the council. This would, however, exclude anyone who was involved in the handling of the cases then before the Children's Hearings. Mr McCallum said that the representatives the Committee could meet would, of course, have no detailed knowledge of the cases, and would only be able to speak in general terms. He added that the Social Work Department could not be represented at such a meeting.

The Parents' Action Committee was continually frustrated in its attempts to seek a dialogue with the Council. The offer by Mr

McCallum seemed pointless. There were several other matters of concern, and they attempted to hold discussions, or to get answers to their questions.

On 29 March they wrote again to Paul Lee. By this time, they were looking ahead to the long-term effects on the children of the arbitrary manner in which they had been removed, and the lengthy absence from their homes and families.

They wrote to the Director to ask for consideration to be given to the rehabilitation and counselling of the nine on their return home. The committee felt strongly that preparations should be put in hand immediately to offer such counselling to the children whenever their return might be. If the plans were laid, then they could be put into effect as soon as the children came home.

They asked for a multi-agency conference to be convened, involving the Social Work Department, teachers, doctors and health visitors. They pointed out that local personnel in these fields had no experience in long term caring for such children, and they added that such a conference should be convened without delay, as leaving it until the children were returned home would be too late. No action was taken.

Meantime, the Parents' Action Committee had been writing letters to Councillors as well. On 14 March they wrote to every Orkney Island councillor, outlining the situation to date, and sending a full copy of the PAIN report and details of the formation of the support group. They were asking the elected members to read the report, reconsider the issues surrounding the whole affair, and assist them in getting some answers from the council officials.

The responses were varied. Some councillors expressed their deep concern, but declined to comment further; some promised help and support, and expressed their own outrage at the course of events; some didn't take the trouble to answer the letter at all. A few of them, however, proceeded to make their own enquiries. The local member for South Ronaldsay and Burray, Councillor Cyril Annal, wrote to Orkney Health Board asking whether there had been any consultation with Health Board employees and general practitioners prior to the removal of the nine children from their homes. The reply from the Board's General Manager, Dr James Cromarty, was unequivocal. There had been no such consultation. Mr Annal wrote, too, to the Education Department, to discover for himself whether the children's teachers had ever been consulted. Again the answer came as no surprise. Neither the Education Department as a whole, nor the Child Psychology section, had been consulted in these matters. This reply, however, turned out to be incorrect, as teachers had been asked for pen-portraits of the children for use at the Panel Hearings, and the Acting Director of Education Mike Drever had supported the request.

Councillor Fiona Matheson from Stromness, a member of the Social Work Committee, consistently pressed for information. She asked the Chief Executive for clarification of the policy for taking children into care. In the absence of the Orkney guidelines, she asked to be told which guidelines had been used, and whether these had *ever* been placed before the Island's Social Work Committee for their approval. Councillor Matheson also asked if any social workers presently in the employ of Orkney Islands Council had at any time in their careers, attended conferences, seminars or other courses organised by the Reachout Trust? She stressed that, as a councillor and member of the Social Work Committee, it was important that she should be in possession of these facts as soon as possible.

In his reply, the Chief Executive told Councillor Matheson that the Social Work Department had been in the process of compiling guidelines when 'the present difficulties' arose. Therefore, he said, formal guidelines for Orkney had not been submitted to the committee.

Mr Gilbert said the department had received guidance from the Scottish Office, and had access to guidelines used by other local authorities. He added, though, that there were *no* guidelines to cover the situation which had manifested itself in Orkney, and even if the council had formally adopted written guidelines, they would not have been appropriate in the circumstances. He concluded by saying that, as far as he was aware, none of the council's social workers had attended any courses of instruction organised by the Reachout Trust.

Councillor Matheson was not satisfied. She considered it very remiss of the Social Work Department not to inform the Social Work Committee of what guidelines or policy it intended to use as a stop gap measure. There had been a committee meeting on 20 February, only seven days before the children were taken away. She felt sure that plans must have been well advanced for the action they intended to take, and she thought that councillors should have been asked to approve the use of emergency guidelines at that time. No hint of what was to come was given at that meeting on 20 February. Councillors serving on the Social Work Committee were as shocked by events a week later as everyone else.

In a further letter to the Chief Executive, Councillor Matheson said that, had emergency guidelines been approved by the committee, the department could have acted in the knowledge that its committee had backed their use. She believed the department had left itself extremely vulnerable in acting without any form of approval by the committee. This, she said, left her unable to support the actions of the Social Work Department, and extremely concerned that they had acted too hastily in a situation that was not of life-threatening proportions to the children involved.

Mrs Matheson also pursued the question of the Temporary Press Officer appointed by Orkney Islands Council. She sought to discover where he had obtained the information he was supposed to have passed on to a Sunday newspaper. She was informed, as was everyone else in the council statement, that Mr Clayton would have had no access to the sort of information quoted in the paper. Nick Clayton himself denied he had ever said the things relating to medical evidence that had been quoted. He accused the newspaper of making them up.

Councillor Spencer Rosie, who had so consistently championed the cause of the suspended Children's Panel Reporter, Katherine Kemp, also gave his whole-hearted backing to the parents' fight. He welcomed the PAIN report, saying it raised issues to be tackled both locally and nationally. He stated categorically that he had no doubts that the parents in this case were innocent.

Councillor Rosie also voiced his concerns over the treatment of the W family, eight members of which had been held in care since November 1990, at enormous cost to Orkney. He was worried that the media might be making too much of the religious implications, and not the real issues at hand. He offered Helen Martini, as Chairman of the Parents' Action Committee, whatever help he could in the campaign to get the children home, and to ensure that a full judicial inquiry was held.

He further stated his concerns by forwarding a paper to the Action Committee for their information. This paper had been given to all councillors by an official of Orkney Islands Council. It was by Roland Summit, a child psychiatrist based in California in the United States, who had been described in one newspaper

article as being discredited. Roland Summit believed fervently in
satanic ritual abuse, and followed the theory that, if a child denies
abuse, that is sufficient evidence that they *have* been abused, and
therefore they should be pushed until they break down and admit it.
This was the reading matter considered suitable for Orkney Islands
councillors, to enable them to understand what was taking place in
their community.

Councillor Rosie was appalled that the paper was American,
outlining aspects of child abuse, what to look for, and how to
confirm suspicions; it was also nearly ten years old, written by
an 'expert' who had been discredited in his own country, and
certainly didn't signify that the council was keeping itself up to
date on matters of such importance.

These, then, were some of Orkney's councillors who weren't
afraid to speak out, who were glad to be seen to be supporting the
stricken families. Others kept their heads down, and others were
openly hostile. They adopted what was becoming the catch-phrase
of the moment – 'if you knew what we know' – but, as even the
Convener of Orkney Islands Council, Jackie Tait, said he did not
know the full details, how did some of the other councillors purport
to know?

CHAPTER TEN

The Proof Hearing

The date for the Proof Hearing to begin had been set for Wednesday 3 April. This was the hearing before the Sheriff taken to the court by acting Orkney Reporter, Gordon Sloan, following the refusal of the parents involved to accept the grounds of referral to the Children's Panel. As had been agreed by the Court of Session on 26 March, it would take place in both Kirkwall and Inverness. The Sheriff to hear the proof was named as Aberdeen Sheriff, David Kelbie.

Before the Proof Hearing began, however, Sheriff Kelbie had to hear the parents' appeal against the continued Place of Safety orders agreed by the Children's Panel on Monday 25 March. The appeal was heard in Kirkwall Sheriff Courthouse on Friday 29 March, which was Good Friday, and under normal circumstances a court holiday. Because the Easter holiday would put it off too long, Sheriff Kelbie agreed that it should be heard on that day, and the four families once more travelled north across the Churchill Barriers towards Kirkwall, to appeal against the Place of Safety orders that kept their children in care on mainland Scotland.

Again, members of the press corps gathered outside. It was a cool, windy day and no one really expected the Sheriff to uphold the parents' appeals. There was no surprise when he did not. It was just another step in the process of law, and the parents and their advisers felt they must use every step available to them.

A huge box of daffodils was delivered while the parents were in the Court. It had come for the four mothers, from a complete stranger who grew daffodils commercially in Cornwall. Moved by the story of their children, and wanting to show support in whatever way possible, the grower sent the flowers to a contact in Orkney, asking that they should be delivered.

They were the first sign of spring in Orkney. The local daffodils had only just poked the tips of their spiky leaves through the cold ground. The heady scent when the lid came off the box seemed to hold out a message of hope, and the mixture of pale and vivid yellow flowers certainly brought with them a message of hope and support from the other end of the United Kingdom. Sheriff Kelbie had agreed with the Children's Panel that there were sound reasons why the nine children should remain in care, and upheld the Place of Safety orders.

So Easter came and went. A time for fun and children, but these four families had no one to share the fun with. For the nine children, separated from their families, there were no cards or chocolate eggs, no loving messages from home, or even from relatives living in other parts of the country. No contact at all with anything or anyone familiar. It was a sad Easter for all of them.

An older daughter of one of the families had asked to be allowed to visit her two young brothers. A law student at a Scottish university, she also queried why she had never been approached by the police or interviewed about her home and family. Although away in term time she was close to her family and spent all her university holidays at home on the farm in South Ronaldsay. Because of the serious nature of the allegations against her parents she said she expected to be questioned, but it didn't happen, and despite her requests, she was not allowed access to her brothers. A spokesman for Orkney's Social Work Department said this applied to all relatives. Some of them had asked if they could foster the children, or at the very least be permitted to phone or visit. All were refused.

'No relative is getting access to the children due to the serious nature of the information given to the social workers,' was the reason given by the Department for keeping the children in isolation.

Even an attempt to allow Orkney and Shetland MP Jim Wallace to visit the children, in the words of one of the mothers, 'just to give them an Easter hug and let them feel they have not been forgotten', was unsuccessful. No one was to be allowed to have even a tenuous contact with the children, who remained in their separate foster homes, not even in touch with each other. Older siblings, returning to Orkney for the Easter holiday, were not allowed to visit the children in care; nor were they permitted to send taped messages to them.

Now all the parents' hopes were pinned on the Proof Hearing. They welcomed the opportunity to have the evidence led, and to hear exactly what lay behind the sordid allegations which had been made against them. The Reporter to the Children's Panel, Gordon Sloan, and the Social Work Department, believed the Proof Hearing would completely vindicate them, and prove that the action they had taken had been the right – indeed the only – thing to do.

On Tuesday 2 April the two solicitors acting for the four families, John Moir and Alastair Bruce, told the press that the proceedings would be in private. No details of any evidence given before the court would be revealed, they said. Already the press and media representatives were bound by the ruling that says no children may be identified. This of course means that their parents, families and homes may not be identified either. The press had stuck to this, referring only to 'one father' or 'one family'. Photographs, however, had edged nearer the bounds of what was permissible. Newspapers and television had shown back views of all the parents, and they became familiar in identifiable surroundings.

For the Proof Hearing, however, it was made clear that confidentiality was vitally important. Questioned about the alternatives facing Sheriff Kelbie, solicitor Alasdair Bruce said: 'His function is simply to decide whether the facts related to the grounds of referral are proved or not proved. He doesn't decide what to do with the children at the end of the day. If he decides the grounds are proved, then it goes back to the Children's Panel and they decide what to do with the children. If he decides the grounds are *not* proved, then that's the end of the matter; the whole thing is dismissed and the children are returned home.'

That was the outcome the parents were confident they deserved. They approached the day with a feeling of relief that at last they could speak out. They had all felt as if they had been living in a sort of limbo for the past five weeks. One thing, however, worried them all as the day dawned. They feared that their children might be counting on this as the day when they would return home. The parents knew that the case would take much longer than that, and their children's release could still be some time away. They all prayed that their children's hopes and expectations hadn't risen to such a pitch where the disappointment would be devastating, and in the end even more damaging than the separation they were all having to endure.

Their own hopes and expectations were pinned on the fact that they believed they had right on their side. Their emotions, understandably near the surface, had jerked up and down as one day followed another. They said they had managed to keep going solely because of the strength of the support they had received from friends, neighbours and complete strangers.

THE PROOF HEARING 107

On the eve of the Proof Hearing, one of the fathers, Mr M, was asked by journalists how he and his wife had managed to cope so far. He replied: 'With a lot of help from our friends. All the time we have anxiety about whether the Scottish legal system is actually strong enough to cope with a case like this, and our emotions go up and down. It is people's prayers and people's kindness that keep us going. We know we're innocent; our children know we're innocent; the children who've said the things which have been turned into allegations, know we're innocent; everybody around here knows we're innocent. Now the Sheriff has to look at the evidence and decide for himself.'

The extreme importance of the case about to take place was recognised by everyone. On a personal level, it was obviously recognised by the families, supporters and friends; on a wider level by the press and media, who had gathered in strength for the opening of the case in Kirkwall, and on a national level by the lawyers, and the law-makers who were watching events from further afield. All were well aware of the significance of what was taking place in Orkney. It could have immeasurable repercussions on the whole pattern of child care law in Scotland, and it could justify the enormous publicity the case had attracted. Solicitor Alasdair Bruce spoke for them all: 'This is *the* most important case involving children in Scotland, probably ever.'

The morning of Wednesday 3 April dawned cool and breezy. Friends and supporters joined journalists, radio reporters and television crews outside the courthouse in Kirkwall. Children dashed about and played together on the grass beneath the trees between the two ancient palaces. Rooks cawed noisily overhead, and the parents were handed bunches of daffodils by Action Committee members and friends as they followed their legal advisers into the elegant stone-built court.

Despite being aware that these proceedings were to be held in private, some of the press tried to get permission to go inside. They were hardly surprised when this was not forthcoming, and the many local and national press men and women prepared themselves for a lengthy wait.

Meanwhile, representatives from the South Ronaldsay Parents Action Committee used the waiting time to go to the Islands' Social Work Department. They wanted to meet Paul Lee face to face and ask him why the nine children had not received the many letters and cards that they knew had been sent to them from schoolfriends and well-wishers, care of the Social Work Department. The committee and the parents had been told of the non-arrival of mail by their lawyers, who in turn had heard it from the Curators, the lawyers appointed solely to look after the interests of the children in care.

The parents knew of many of the letters that had been sent to their children; they did not know about the avalanche of cards and greetings from well-wishers and strangers all over the country that were not getting through to bring a measure of comfort to the children who were separated from their families and everything familiar in their lives. The Action Committee only sought answers from the department about the letters they knew had been sent.

The Social Work Director told the Action Committee that he was planning to write to the lawyers about the correspondence 'soon'. It was not a comfortable interview on either side, and it certainly did not clear the air on the question of the letters. It was assumed by those supporting the parents that social workers had decided that any correspondence to the children would contain 'trigger words'; that is some sort of code that worked in conjunction with rituals.

Those who seek to warn the world of such things believe that very simple every-day words can be used for this purpose, and therefore that everyone who writes to a child in these circumstances is, somehow 'in on the plot'. They believe, too, that familiar objects from home, such as much-loved toys or books, can carry the same signals. Paul Lee, however, did not say this to the delegation that met him. He said the letters had been forwarded from his department to those who were in charge of the children in mainland Scotland, and said he would make enquiries.

In the court, Sheriff Kelbie listened to a legal debate on the Children's Hearings which had originally decided the fate of the nine children. He heard counsel for some of the parents put forward the argument that the hearings were incompetent because the children had not been present to be advised of the grounds of referral. He heard that the children's presence had been dispensed with at the behest of the interim acting Reporter to Orkney Children's Panel, Gordon Sloan, and he heard Mr Sloan's QC say that this was justified. The Children's Panel had believed, said the counsel, that they possessed powers to dispense with the children, and she referred to the section of the Social Work (Scotland) Act of 1968, which says that the attendance of a child is not necessary for the just hearing of a case if the Panel are satisfied that it would be detrimental to the interest of a child.

Sheriff Kelbie was not convinced by this argument.

'How could anybody,' he said 'applying their minds to statute and rule, have made a decision not to have the children present because of the traumatic experience it would create for them?'

The Sheriff was highly critical of the fact that it seemed to have become customary for the rules that were laid down by law to be ignored.

'If that is so,' he said, 'then it is time it was stopped.'

Then came the first surprise of an astounding two days. The Hearing that began, as the lawyers had said it would, in private, was opened up to the press and media reporters in the afternoon, on the instructions of Sheriff Kelbie.

Journalists heard him criticise the procedures of the Children's Panel, and announce that he would consider the handling of the case overnight. He would decide whether this had been done competently, and issue his judgement at ten o'clock the next morning.

If he decided to proceed with the hearing of evidence, he told the court, he would then adjourn the case until the following Monday, when it would continue in Inverness. There, he would meet the children one at a time in his Chambers. He told the parents that it might be possible for them to be reunited with their children after he had met them, but before the children gave their evidence. He asked them to be patient and not to try to contact their children *before* he had met them.

The parents were overjoyed at the prospects of seeing their sons and daughters the following Monday. Their joy, though, was tinged with apprehension. One mother feared that it might not be good for the children to see their parents very briefly before giving evidence. She said it would be very unsettling for them. Their meeting with Sheriff Kelbie was important, and she thought it would be better to meet afterwards. The Curators, however, working with psychologists, would ultimately decide what was really in the best interests of the children in the circumstances, and the parents were happy to abide by their decision.

'Isn't it terrible,' asked the same mother, 'when you have to ask a psychologist if it will be all right for you to hug your child?'

When the parents emerged to face the eager questions of the

waiting journalists they looked tired and drawn, but there was no doubting their relief that the proceedings were under way at last. They were all full of gratitude that it was Sheriff David Kelbie who was to judge their case. Here, at last, they believed, was someone who was prepared to really *listen* to what they had to say. They, and their lawyers, felt that for the first time, the parents were considered to be important, and what they had to say in their defence really mattered.

None of them faced the next day with certainty, but they did face it with the comforting knowledge that they were being given a fair hearing. They had no way of knowing that the events of the next day would make legal history, or that the actions of the Sheriff would be the subject for discussion and debate at every level of society for a very long time.

The journalists, however, having been allowed into the courtroom on the Wednesday afternoon, scented something unusual in the air, and the atmosphere was charged with anticipation as they all met again on Thursday morning. This time they were allowed to go straight in, and make their way up the curved staircase to the courtroom. No cameras or recorders were permitted, but this is normal procedure in courts of law and no one expected them to be. Notebooks and pens were poised and ready; colleagues compared notes so far and speculated on the outcome of the day's proceedings to come.

Two long rows at the back of the small courtroom were packed with reporters. The court was never designed to deal with a case of this magnitude. It simply wasn't big enough to hold everyone who crowded in. In front of the journalists sat the four sets of parents, and every other available space was filled with lawyers.

There were two solicitors, four Queen's Counsel and four junior counsel for the families; four Curators for the children – one for each family – and the four counsel for the Curators. In addition, of course, there were the solicitor, QC and junior counsel for the Reporter to the Children's Panel.

The scene was set. An undercurrent of nervous excitement filled the air. No one guessed at the drama that was about to unfold.

The court rose and Sheriff Kelbie entered. Tall and bearded, he brought with him an air of authority. He proceeded at once to say that he didn't usually lose sleep over a case, but that he had done so over this one. As a matter of course he warned the press that they must not identify the families in any way in the reports they published or broadcast. Then he began to go through his judgement, paragraph by paragraph. He referred to sections and sub-sections of the Social Work (Scotland) Act; he quoted previous comparable cases. He said at once that cases like the one before him now, were very emotive and difficult; they were, he continued, distinguished by failure on the part of the Reporter and the Children's Hearing, to follow certain clear rules of procedure.

In respect of the children who should, in Sheriff Kelbie's view, have been present at the Panel Hearings, he chose to highlight their absence by referring solely to the oldest of the nine children, and using him as the example of the way the children had been dealt with.

The oldest child was the fifteen-year-old boy, who had been taken from his home and sent, under a Place of Safety warrant, to a residential school, not a foster home. His parents had been told at a Children's Hearing that he was in a foster home. The failure to have this child at the Hearings was particularly difficult to understand, said the Sheriff.

The Children's Hearing had been satisfied that this boy did not understand the explanation of the grounds of referral to the Panel. These were the grounds that his parents had refused to accept. By that token the Panel had deemed it unnecessary to have him present at the hearings. Sheriff Kelbie said that the statement of the grounds of referral were such that it should not be very difficult for a fifteen-year-old boy to understand. He said no explanation had, in fact, ever been offered to the boy at all.

One of the tasks for the Chairman of a Children's Panel is to explain the grounds of referral to a child of any age in a way suitable to its age, so that the grounds may be easily understood. Most Children's Panels in Scotland adhere to this practice, explaining carefully to children why the procedures are taking place. Exceptions are of course made when a child is an infant, or too young to be able to understand at all, or where there might be problems of understanding due to learning difficulties.

A fifteen-year-old is extremely unlikely to have problems understanding such an explanation. Children much younger than that can understand when the explanations are carefully and sympathetically given, and the fifteen-year-old in question was a bright, intelligent boy, who questioned everything with all the audacity of a teenager who is fast becoming an adult.

Sheriff Kelbie outlined the law regarding the attendance of children at hearings. The law, he said, stated that, where a child is detained under a Place of Safety warrant, then the Reporter 'shall, wherever practicable, arrange a children's hearing to sit not later than in the course of the first lawful day after the commencement of the child's detention to consider the case'. This had not been done.

The Sheriff told the court of the rules concerning 'Form I'. This is a form which must be given to a child as soon as possible before a hearing, giving notification of the hearing, and which points out that the child is required to attend. In fact, it transpired that Form I had indeed been sent to the fifteen-year-old. It had been addressed to him at his parents' home in South Ronaldsay. The home from which the authorities had removed him, and where the Reporter, whose business it was to ensure the form was sent to the child, knew he could not be found.

The Sheriff said it was difficult to understand what function it served, sending the form to the boy's home, unless it was to cause unnecessary distress to the parents. He also said it was quite clear that the hearing had never considered whether this boy was capable of understanding the explanation, let alone satisfied themselves that he was not.

Sheriff Kelbie continued that where the hearing decides that the attendance of the child is not necessary for the just hearing of a case, or that it would be detrimental to the interests of the child to be present, then the whole or part of the case can be considered in the absence of the child. That, however, did not mean that the child should be absent at the outset and not have the grounds of referral explained to him or her in person. Accordingly, said the Sheriff, the child was obliged to be present before the Children's Hearing.

Referring to the case that came before Sheriff Principal Ronald Ireland, who had rejected the parents' first appeal, Sheriff Kelbie said it was clear that the case had not been argued as fully before the Sheriff Principal as it had been before himself. He referred to a hearing held by the Children's Panel on Friday 1 March. At that meeting they had decided to dispense with the presence of the children in advance of the Panel Hearing called for the following Tuesday. Sheriff Kelbie maintained that Sheriff

Principal Ireland's ruling was invalidated because of the decision taken at that preliminary meeting, which had been held completely in private. The parents had not been aware of it.

The Sheriff continued that no point had been made at the appeal that 5 March was not the first lawful day after the start of the children's detention. He understood, he said, that it had been conceded that it had not been practicable to arrange the hearing earlier.

As previously noted, the Social Work (Scotland) Act says the hearing should be held, wherever practicable, on the first working day after a child has been removed from home; in this case in Orkney, it wasn't held until the last possible moment, on the seventh day. Sheriff Kelbie, referring to the fact that these matters had not been brought up before the Sheriff Principal, said he seemed only to have dealt with the merits of the appeal.

The decision taken on 1 March by the Panel was, he said, totally illegal. The Reporter's counsel had explained to the hearing that this was common practice. If this was so, said the Sheriff, then in his view it had no validity whatsoever. If the meeting of the Panel on 1 March was a hearing, then it wasn't properly convened in that no notification had been given to children or parents, and the former were not present. If it was not a hearing, then its decisions were of no effect, and decisions had to be taken again at a proper hearing.

In his view, said the Sheriff, the hearing never put itself into a position of directing an application to the Sheriff to hear the proof. Therefore, he said, these applications were incompetent. He referred to a passage from the report on the Cleveland Case which had been quoted to him: 'It is important to remember that children are persons too, and not simply subjects of concern.'

'It appears to me,' said Sheriff Kelbie, 'that if the Reporter and the Hearing had borne that in mind throughout, they would not have failed to appreciate the importance of sticking to the rules, and, indeed, why they are there.'

Sheriff Kelbie was obviously conscious of the difficulties that would ensue whatever his ruling should be. He said it wasn't at all clear who would be benefited by dismissal. He must have been well aware that the parents themselves had welcomed the opportunity to have the evidence heard, and the chance to clear their names.

These were, however, proceedings involving the welfare of children and decisions, he said, had to be taken speedily, and without too much regard for the 'niceties of procedure'. He warned the court that if he dismissed the applications, he couldn't order the children to be brought back home. The warrants to detain them in a Place of Safety would remain in force, and it was open to the Reporter to seek to start the whole case again. In that way, he said, the distress of the children and their parents would simply be prolonged, and really it would be better to have the evidence examined as soon as possible.

He was, though, equally concerned about the other side of the coin, the reputation of the Children's Hearing System under the Social Work (Scotland) Act. It was, he said, justly admired throughout the world as a quick, fair and sympathetic way of dealing with the problems of children.

'It can only continue so if the basic rules are obeyed and the fundamental rights of children observed,' said the Sheriff. 'It will not do if a cavalier attitude is adopted as to whether they are observed or not.'

The Sheriff spoke about the lack of unanimity by the counsel for the parents or the curators. Some had wanted the point of competency pressed; others did not, but wanted to see the whole case drawn to a speedy conclusion on the evidence. Then he spoke the words that electrified the whole courtroom: 'Reluctantly, for the reasons I have already given, I have come to the conclusion that these proceedings are so fatally flawed as to be incompetent.'

The proceedings had been instigated by the Children' Panel, who had had no option but to go to the court for proof after the parents refused to accept the grounds of referral. The Reporter to the Children's Panel, Gordon Sloan, made the applications for proof to be heard by the Sheriff. But Sheriff David Kelbie did not, after all, hear the proof. The expert witnesses were not called, the parents did not get their chance to defend themselves against the allegations.

The Sheriff had, he said, no discretion to allow the proceedings to continue, once it had been decided that they were fundamentally null and void. Accordingly, he dismissed the applications.

There was a moment's complete silence as Sheriff Kelbie paused. Everyone in the room sat up and leant forward; one mother looked as if she might leap over the seat in front of her; every eye was on the man on the bench.

Many of those eyes filled with tears – and it wasn't just those of the parents. They really began to believe they would soon be reunited with their children.

Some of the hard-bitten, cynical journalists had suspiciously bright eyes, too. Many had suffered with the bereft parents, and while always trying to allow the authorities to have their say, and to remain open-minded about the truth of the case, they had steadfastly maintained that the whole affair had been mishandled from the start. Now, it seemed, their publicly stated views had been vindicated.

There, it would seem, the matter rested; but Sheriff David Kelbie endorsed his reputation for being 'his own man', a 'no-nonsense but fair judge'. In doing what he did next, he laid himself open to criticism in many quarters; he may even have damaged his career. This is a man who is so honest he must speak out on issues he believes to be important, regardless of the personal consequences, and speak out he certainly did.

CHAPTER ELEVEN

The Sheriff Continues

After dismissing the applications for the Proof Hearing, that would normally have been the end of the matter – at least as far as the session in the court was concerned. Reporters were ready to leave to file their copy, and to tell the crowd waiting outside in the cold spring morning about the dramatic events they had missed.

It was not over yet, however. Sheriff David Kelbie had not yet finished all he wanted to say. Not afraid of expressing his views in a forthright manner, he continued to comment on the case, and in doing so astounded all those who heard him. In dismissing the applications, he said, he had done sufficient to dispose of the matter before him, but in view of the importance of the case, and the nine children being detained, he could not, in all conscience, leave matters in that unsatisfactory state without further comment.

He began by referring back to the appeals by the parents which he had heard the previous Friday. The four sets of parents had appealed against the continuation of the Place of Safety warrants on their children, and he had dismissed their appeals. The Sheriff said he had believed then that the hearing had not properly fulfilled its duty to consider the interests of the children and to balance the risks of harm to them in deciding whether or not to renew the warrants. He had not, however, been able to get from QC Lynda Clarke, counsel for the Reporter, or Gordon Sloan, the interim Reporter all the information he would have preferred to have before reaching a decision on the appeals.

On balance, and because the date of the Proof Hearing was so close, he had therefore decided not to disturb the status quo. He had upheld the decision of the Children's Panel and the nine children had remained in care, somewhere in mainland Scotland.

Sheriff Kelbie then went on to say that although he realised he was not in a position now to review that decision, the Social Work Department were not obliged to continue to enforce a twenty-one day warrant if it ceased to perform a useful function. He said matters had changed a great deal since Friday, and then he dropped a bombshell which shook everyone in the court. If he had known the previous Friday what he knew now, he said, he would have granted the parents' appeals and the children would have returned home.

One of the changes, of course, was the fact that the proof would not now be heard soon, as he had dismissed the applications. He told the hushed courtroom that he had also spent the last few days – and it would seem, nights, too – considering most of the documentary productions in the case, and in particular he had read all the transcripts of interviews with the children, and had listened to the tapes of all the crucial interviews. These had evidently had a profound effect on the Sheriff.

He said he had become very aware that the nine children had been held without any contact with any of their families or friends, under the Place of Safety warrants. He added that, far from being kept in a place of safety, the children had repeatedly been taken to another place altogether to be subjected to what the Sheriff said could only be called cross-examination designed to make them break down and admit to being abused.

He was referring to the interview sessions conducted by personnel from the Royal Scottish Society for the Prevention of Cruelty to Children. They were responsible for interviewing the three W children from whose statements the allegations had been made, and they also interviewed the nine children taken from their homes on 27 February.

Following Sheriff Kelbie's statement that he would have returned the children home the previous Friday if he'd been in possession of the information he now had to hand, a gasp was heard round the courtroom. Reporters could only guess at the sort of cross-examination he meant, and there was a shudder of horror at the thought of young children being subjected to such treatment, particularly by those whose justification was always that 'it was in the best interests of the children'.

Sheriff Kelbie said that children could, of course, be visited in the places of safety to which they had been sent, and asked there to talk about what had happened to them; but he said that in his view there was no lawful authority for what had happened in this case, with the children being removed for questioning.

He was, he said, glad to hear Mr Sloan's QC, Lynda Clarke, say that when she realised this was happening, she had advised that it should stop, but what had happened before her intervention, he said, was yet another example of failure to regard the children as persons possessed of rights.

The Sheriff described Miss Clarke's handling of the case as sympathetic and sensible, and filled with difficulties not of her making. She had, he said, told him on the previous Friday – the day the parents had made their appeal against the Place of Safety warrants – that the information on which the allegations had been based had come from three children who had suffered serious sexual abuse and who were undergoing 'disclosure therapy'. The Sheriff said that after some time these three children had spontaneously produced stories of a similar kind involving the sort of allegations in the grounds of referral. Two of the other nine children were said to have made allegations which supported the story.

Further surprising the hushed courtroom, Sheriff Kelbie continued. He knew he hadn't heard the proof, he said, but in the interests of the children he felt he had to express a view on these matters. He did not feel competent to judge whether what had been going on with the first three children was a form of therapy, but he was very clear about the fact that it was not the way to get at the truth objectively. He said the statements by these three children could not be said to be spontaneous. Their answers, he said, had clearly shown that they had been subjected to or witnessed sexual abuse, but there was no doubting that this had happened within their own family.

The Sheriff drew attention to the fact that the disclosures in question were first made during interviews in February – shortly before the other nine children were taken from their homes at seven o'clock in the morning. There were no tapes or full transcripts of these interviews, he said, and no indication of the questions which had elicited the children's statements. Because of the manner of questioning in the other transcripts, however, Sheriff Kelbie said there would be great difficulty in assessing how reliable the statements were.

Turning to the statements from the two other children who had apparently made allegations to support the story of the first three, the Sheriff said that certainly two of them had said things which bore a marked similarity to certain things said by those children.

Sheriff Kelbie continued to criticise the system used to get at the information, saying these statements had been made with the active encouragement of those conducting the interviews, who were clearly determined to get a particular response. He said the manner of interviewing all the children amounted to repeated coaching of a kind which would not only have made the record of the interviews of doubtful value, but he thought they may well have tainted anything they said in court.

In any event, said the Sheriff, the two later children said absolutely nothing to show that they had experienced or seen any sexual abuse, ritual or otherwise. In fact one of them had categorically stated that it had never happened to her, and that she had never seen it happen to anyone else, and Sheriff Kelbie said it was clear that what she was describing was something she had discussed with one of the first three children at an earlier date. The first children had indeed experienced abuse; they were three members of a family of fifteen whose father was serving a jail sentence for the physical and sexual abuse of his children.

Sheriff Kelbie described as 'of far more significance' the fact that the other seven of the nine children taken into care in February 1991, emphatically and convincingly denied that anything had ever happened, and equally significantly stated that those interviewing them were not prepared to listen to that.

The Sheriff said that even the first three children didn't stick to their stories, which, although they contained similarities, also contained marked variations. One of them, he said, quite clearly stated at one point during interview: 'No. Did you know this was all a lie?' but the remark was brushed aside.

The Sheriff told the court that even if their evidence was accepted in full, he was not clear just what it would have proved, and he added that, judging from the vague nature of the statement in the grounds of referral to the Children's Panel, neither was the Reporter clear about that.

Continuing to look at the tapes and transcripts, Sheriff Kelbie said the stories bore certain similarities to each other, but also to Christmas and Halloween parties and a wedding described by the other children. There were also significant discrepancies. He found it difficult to be sure about what was meant in the grounds of referral by 'ritualistic music'. Depending on which child was telling the story, he said, it was either Kylie Minogue, Michael Jackson, possibly Andrew Lloyd Webber's *Phantom of the Opera*, the *Strip the Willow*, or *The Grand Old Duke of York*. He said that, so far as the children from the H and M families in particular were concerned, one of the first three children had, with considerable encouragement, added them to a list of people present at an unspecified event.

Proceeding to mention the objects removed from the houses of the four families and the minister, Sheriff Kelbie said he was aware of these being lodged as productions, and included a cloak, masks, crosses and unusual statuary, but he said the items appeared to him to have little evidential significance, unless one had started off to see it. In fact the Sheriff was voicing in public what so many people had been saying to each other – that there was nothing sinister in any of the items removed from the houses which had been searched, unless a certain significance had been actively pursued.

He did not dismiss the statements of the first three children completely out of hand, however. He didn't intend to say there was nothing in the statements of those children worthy of further investigation, but what it was and how it should be investigated was not, in Sheriff Kelbie's opinion, clear.

Whatever the truth of the matter, however, and putting what the first three children had said at its highest, the Sheriff said he was in no doubt that the risks to the welfare of the nine children in returning them to their parents were far outweighed by the certain damage being done by their continued detention, and that the sooner they were returned to their parents the better.

Concluding the statement which had held everyone in the crowded courtroom completely spellbound, the Sheriff referred to the Reporter, who was not in the court. He said that if the Reporter was still considering taking the matter further, he hoped he would give very serious consideration – in relation to each child separately – to just what was the nature and quality of the evidence he relied on, the manner in which it was obtained, and perhaps also to the wealth of contrary evidence, before he did so.

Smiles of delight mingled with tears of relief as the stunned reporters, the families and their legal representatives left the court, and took the news to the patiently waiting crowd outside. A little group of supporters gathered round each journalist to hear the story at first hand, and when the parents emerged there were joyful hugs from those who had waited for just such news. No one had expected this course of events, and none of them knew what would happen next. They knew that the Sheriff had no power to bring the children home. He had only said he hoped this would now be done. But it was up to the Reporter and the Social Work Department of Orkney

Islands Council to make the decision, and make the arrangements to carry it out.

When Sheriff Kelbie emerged quietly from the courthouse a spontaneous cheer rang out. He spoke to no one, but there was the suggestion of a smile on his face as he left the precincts of the court. Already people were describing his decision to throw the case out as a brave one; the actions of a kind and honest man who was moved by the suffering of children, but actions which might have repercussions at a later date. One of the mothers said: 'Thank God for the Sheriff. This is a victory for commonsense. It has taken the Sheriff just two days to discover what we have known for five weeks – that the kids should never have been taken away.'

As members of the South Ronaldsay Parents Action Committee welcomed the news, and put their arms around the parents of the nine missing children, the first excitement began to turn to anger. Within minutes the parents and their supporters decided to go at once to the Social Work Department to see the director, Paul Lee. They wanted to know immediately when and how their children would be returned to them. The Committee Chairman Dr Helen Martini told waiting reporters that if the council had organised a plane to fly the children out of the island in such a hurry, they could just as easily organise one to bring them back, and they would demand just that.

About sixty people marched the couple of hundred yards or so to Orkney Islands Council headquarters in the next street. Led by the eight parents they burst into Paul Lee's office. A receptionist tried to hold them back, but the emotion, kept in check for five agonising weeks, burst out, and nothing would have stopped them from facing the man they held personally responsible for their pain.

With the team leader Sue Miller, beside him, Paul Lee stood behind his desk, his face grim and pale. The families and supporters who packed into the office seemed menacing. One of the mothers said she hoped they were a little bit frightened, but even if they were it wouldn't be nearly enough, she said, as the children had been frightened when they were taken from their homes. When Sue Miller lifted a telephone receiver to call the police, the same mother pushed her hand down onto the phone to stop her; there were emotional claims of injury and threats of legal action against the mother for assault.

The parents accused the social work director of stealing their children, of interrogating them illegally, and of having medical examinations carried out without parental consent. They demanded the immediate return of the nine children, and the resignation of Paul Lee. All the frustrations and despair of the past nine weeks tumbled out in bitter recriminations.

The police were called, and they arrived on the scene very quickly from the police station attached to the rear of the court building. By this stage, however, the anger had abated somewhat, and the Action Committee members and supports agreed to leave Paul Lee's office. No arrests were made, and only the parents remained inside. Later one mother emerged to say that Mr Lee had told her that the children would be returned to Orkney before nightfall if possible. There were difficulties involved, as the children were scattered across Scotland.

Meanwhile Orkney Islands Council's Chairman, Councillor Jackie Tait told reporters that he would personally organise a charter plane to collect the children and bring them home. They would definitely, he said, be back in Orkney before dark. In the middle of the afternoon the council issued a formal statement saying the children would be returned home as soon as possible, and a similar one came from the Reporter to the Children's Panel. It was open to him to re-start the whole case. The Place of Safety warrants were still valid, after all, but he agreed at that time to support the children's homecoming.

No one knew quite what to do next. Should they go home and prepare for the arrival, or stay in Kirkwall until it was time to go out to the tiny airport? The next few hours were anxious ones, as it wasn't yet certain whether the logistics of gathering up the nine children from eight different locations and bringing them back to Orkney could be accomplished by nightfall. As the plane wouldn't be able to land after dark, there was still the possibility that the children might have to stay away from home for one more night.

At last the families, reporters, television cameras, photographers and what seemed like the whole population of South Ronaldsay drove the three short miles out to Kirkwall Airport. They packed the tiny air terminal building, and the excitement was at fever pitch. The parents themselves were taken through to the customs room where they would be able to greet their children in private, away from the glare of publicity, and the exuberant welcome of the people who had supported them for the five endless weeks.

At eight minutes past seven that wet and windy Thursday evening, the plane carrying the nine children from South Ronaldsay touched down on Orkney soil. It seemed like hours, but was only a few minutes before the steps were in place and the children tumbled out and ran joyously across the tarmac to where their parents were waiting. And the children who had left the island five weeks and one day before, without a single personal possession, now came home with their hands clutching carrier bags full of clothes, toys and gifts from their foster homes.

The tears and the emotion of those first precious moments of reunion can only be imagined. The privacy in which to cherish those first tender embraces was something which the parents were more than grateful for. It gave them a few moments in which to reach out and touch their beloved children, a few moments to make sure they were really there, and basically alright. The effects of the trauma would come later; for now it was enough just to have and to hold.

Then it was time to brave the warm and happy welcome inside the airport building. A piper was playing *Scotland the Brave* 'to welcome the bairns home'; there were flowers for everyone, balloons, streamers, cheers, laughter and excited chatter. The gathering of reporters, television cameras and photographers, sometimes an inhibiting factor, did nothing to dampen the high spirits – in fact they, too, were touched by and involved in the warmth of the welcome home. Everyone wanted to talk to the children, even to put out a hand and touch them, just to make sure they were really back in Orkney.

One little boy said he was looking forward to riding his bike again; another, a little older, waved happily to classmates from school who had come to the airport to share in the celebration. One father, Mr M, asked how he thought his children were, said they seemed to be relatively all right, but time would tell how they really were after the experience they had been through. Then, as certain well-wishers in the know started to sing 'Happy Birthday', he admitted it was indeed his birthday and the very best one he could ever remember in his whole life.

Commenting on the sheer agony of the previous five weeks, he said the worst part had been not knowing about the welfare of the children, and having no faith in the system.

The joyous welcome over, the families wanted only one thing; to get home, and there, in the privacy and security of familiar surroundings, to begin their lives all over again. They knew that the children would begin to talk about their five weeks away, about their experiences and their feelings; they didn't know when this process would start, and they had no professional counselling to help them to help their children. They left the airport and the still cheering crowds, with their arms tightly around their children as if they were scared they might suddenly be taken away again.

CHAPTER TWELVE

What the Children Said

So Sheriff Kelbie's ruling that the case was 'fatally flawed' had resulted in the nine children returning to their homes in Orkney. Their emotions as they drove south across the dramatic Churchill Barriers, with Scapa Flow's deep waters on one side and the North Sea on the other, can only be guessed at. That they were happy and excited to be back was easy to see, but what, if any, psychological damage had been done to these children was not. The parents could only be glad to have them home, and wait until the children themselves felt they could talk about their experiences during those five isolated weeks.

Eagerly the gathered reporters waited to see if the children would talk to them. They didn't have to wait long. A senior child psychiatrist from Manchester advised the parents to let the children talk to the press – *if they wanted to*. No pressure, she urged, should be put on the children by anyone, but if they felt like talking, then she judged it would be therapeutic for them. Some of the children themselves approached the reporters and offered to talk about the situation they had found themselves in five weeks and two days earlier.

It was inevitable that many of the national press wanted to talk to the oldest child first of all. At fifteen, the older of the two M boys to be taken from home, he was most likely to be articulate, and probably the most angry. When he heard his mother shouting at someone on the stairs early that February morning, his first instinct was to get up and 'do a runner'. On second thoughts he stayed so that his eleven-year-old brother wouldn't have to face whatever was to come, alone.

In the end, each of them had to face the situation alone, as did seven of the nine; only two sisters were allowed to be together. They were all driven from their homes to Kirkwall. Some were taken to Camoran, the children's home, others to different locations where they waited for a couple of hours until it was time to go to the airport to board the specially chartered plane that would fly them away from their island homes, and their families.

The fifteen-year-old waited until a social worker came to get him. He washed and dressed and said goodbye to his mother, which the police tried to stop. He and his brother were then taken in the same car to Kirkwall. On the way there, the social worker, who identified himself as being from the RSSPCC said this would just be for one day, as they wanted to ask them some questions, and he told them they would be together. This proved to be untrue, as the boys weren't even allowed to sit together on the plane. Each child was accompanied by a social worker, and no conversation between the children was permitted.

The plane flew first to Inverness, where five of the children were taken off, including the fifteen-year-old's younger brother. The boys hugged each other to say goodbye, but were pulled apart by a social worker. Then the plane continued its journey to Glasgow. On the way there, the RSSPCC social worker told the boy it would be a week before anything happened. He explained the case would come up at the Orkney Children's Panel, and he could then be kept in care for a further twenty-one days. The fifteen-year-old said the social worker obviously expected him to be away for at least that long, as he planned to see him at various times during that period.

The boy said that no explanation of the reason for his removal from home was given. 'They said "abuse" and that was it. They just shut up after that. I only found out about the ritual stuff and the sexual stuff because I saw it later in the paper. They didn't tell me any of that.'

When the plane arrived in Glasgow, the remaining children had to wait on board until cars were brought to the steps to collect them. They were then driven straight to a Glasgow hospital for medical examinations. The oldest boy, questioning this, was told he had no legal right to refuse, he had to be examined, and it was only afterwards he was told the doctors had been looking for signs of abuse. He didn't, however, blame the doctors for the situation he found himself in; 'they were only doing their job, but it wasn't very pleasant'.

This boy, whose parents were later told at the Childrens Hearing in Kirkwall that he was with foster parents, was then driven into Ayrshire, to Geilsland Residential School, where he was to spend the next five weeks. The RSSPCC social worker and police drove him to the school and left him there, in the boy's own words 'to start again, they hoped'.

Geilsland was more of a residential college than a school, the boys there aged between fifteen and eighteen. All of them were placed with the school through their local Social Work Departments, the majority on orders from Childrens Panels, some through Sheriff Court Orders and a few were in care on a voluntary basis.

The school is run by the Church of Scotland Board of Social Responsibility, which is the largest voluntary social work agency in Scotland. Its aim is to complete each boy's formal education and prepare them for employment or further training. The majority of the boys had been through damaging childhood experiences, such as abuse, deprivation and disruption. Many had been in other placements previously – foster homes, children's homes, other schools, and many had a pattern of offending.

When the parents of the fifteen-year-old boy first learnt he might be in what they thought was a 'List D' school and not, in fact, in a foster home, they contacted Orkney's Social Work Chairman, Councillor Mairhi Trickett, and asked her if it was true. She came back and told them that their son was in a residential school; she had been told by Sam Mactaggart of the RSSPCC that there were no 'List D' schools any more, but she didn't mention that it had formerly been a 'List D' school. She assured them that their son was 'fine'.

When his story was first told in the newspapers, there was an outcry. This was an innocent boy, the stories told, who had been put into a school for child offenders, many of whom were waiting to go to court, and he had learnt there how to steal cars and take drugs. The reality was very different. The boy said the other boys were in the school for a variety of reasons, and only a few, he believed were waiting to go to court.

In idle conversation, he said, he had found out how to roll a joint, and some of the boys had talked about breaking into cars, but they had actually taught him nothing. He thought the press had exaggerated the situation unnecessarily. He had liked most of the other boys, and he had certainly liked the staff at the school. They were good to him; they brought in the newspapers so he could read for himself what was going on in Orkney, what was happening to his family and the families of the other children taken from their homes at the same time. They let him watch the news reports on television, too, and were willing to listen to him, to talk about the case, and, he said, to believe him. The social worker from the RSSPCC, who frequently took him away for questioning, didn't, he said, believe a word.

For the first ten days, he was take away for questioning every other day, then it became less often for the remainder of the five weeks he was away. He was questioned by a policewoman, and a male social worker from the Society. They wanted to know if anything had happened to him? He told them no, nothing had. They asked if he had witnessed anything happening to any other children. Again, he told them no. Then they asked what he'd say if he knew other children had been saying things? He replied, 'Well, you'd be asking them leading questions.' 'We don't do that sort of thing,' they said. Yet Sheriff Kelbie, in throwing the proof hearing out of court, said the manner of interviewing all the children amounted to repeated coaching. He said the children had made statements with the active encouragement of those conducting the interviews, who were clearly determined to get a particular response.

The oldest boy said his interviewers hadn't tried to make him say any particular thing, but they simply hadn't believed his repeated denials of abuse to himself or other children. One session, he said, was spent talking about his feelings. He was asked to say how he felt when he was removed from his home, and how he felt now, and what other experiences he'd had that gave him the same sort of feelings. Another session was devoted to his childhood; where he'd lived, what he could remember, and he had been told to draw a plan of his old house. This line of questioning was puzzling, and he had no idea of where it was leading.

In the last few sessions, he said, the tone seemed to change. He was still asked if anything had happened to him, and after his denial, the conversation centred around films, and general chit-chat. He described it as 'just a waste of time'.

Although this was a school, his education was interrupted. On the plane south he asked the social worker what would happen about his schooling, and was told something would be sorted out. He joined the boys of his own age, but found the work was of a much lower standard than he was doing at school in Orkney; 'it was younger work, work my brother could have done. I mean a lot of the boys there hadn't been to school since they were twelve or thirteen, so it was fair enough, but for me it was too easy.' After some considerable time, some English work was sent to him from school in Kirkwall, but only, he said, because his teacher had fought to have it sent. It arrived too late for him to make a start on it, and the covering letter sent by the teacher in question had been re-written and all personal references removed. However, when he did get back to school in Orkney, he didn't feel he'd got left too far behind. 'If I'd had a sports injury,' he said, 'I might have been off for longer.'

His parents, though, thought he was finding it more difficult to catch up than he admitted. They said the continuous assessment was the main problem, and that some teachers were making allowances for his enforced absence, others were not.

Summing up his feelings after all that had happened to him, the boy said he'd felt really angry. He still felt angry towards some social workers, the police, and the RSSPCC, and he felt his dealings with authorities in future would be coloured by his experiences. Something needed to be done to the law to stop it ever happening to children again, he said.

'They did have a hell of a cheek. They basically took us to get the evidence. It was all very wrong in the way they did it. I mean, I would have had no complaints whatsoever if they'd just come and talked to us and investigated what they'd heard, but they simply took us away just to back up what they'd heard.'

These were some of the thoughts and feelings of a mature and articulate fifteen-year-old one week after returning home to his parents. He told them it was important to remain angry. 'You've got to keep hating,' he said, 'or your guard will go down and you'll be less alert.' After the questioning was officially stopped, this boy was woken early one morning and taken to the usual interviewing place. This time he was interviewed by two policemen instead of social workers. He'd had no breakfast, and was offered no food or drink throughout the session. They eventually returned him to the school in the afternoon. As a result of what the boy considered to be a 'heavy' interview, he believed there were no good, honest police officers anywhere. His parents later criticised the police interview, and said they thought withholding food was designed to weaken him and encourage him to 'disclose'.

His eleven-year-old brother was more subdued. His parents said his sparkle and mischief had disappeared, and he was being very good. He had regressed, they thought, and become very clingy, needing lots of hugs and constant loving reassurance. His room was unnaturally tidy, and he was afraid of being taken away again. A gentle child, rather young for his eleven years, he had fared well in his foster home.

In an imaginative matching, he had been sent to a farming family, who took him to their hearts, and treated him with affection and consideration. He didn't want to lose touch with them after he returned home.

Sensitive to his bewilderment, and his need to know something of the story that surrounded his removal from his home, his foster family let him watch television, and let him talk and cry. The mother hugged and comforted him. The whole family were kind, caring and understanding. They made him feel very much at home by giving him jobs around the farm – jobs he was familiar with as they were part of his daily life at home. He was sent to the local school, where the head teacher was also sensitive and understanding. He liked the school and his teacher, but when he returned home he found it hard to talk about his experiences, and his parents said that the story emerged bit by bit.

The medical examination upset him most of all. It had taken place a day or two after arriving at Inverness, and he was taken to an RSSPCC centre, not a hospital. The boy found it hard to talk about this episode, even to Val Mellor, the consultant clinical psychiatrist who talked to the children, and had advised the parents to allow them to talk to reporters.

The two children from the T family, a twelve-year-old boy and his eight-year-old sister, asked if they could talk to the press. They talked of their feelings of bewilderment when the social workers arrived in their home at seven o'clock in the morning. The boy said he wanted to run away, but the social workers followed him everywhere, even to the toilet. The little girl – who was later to be described as 'in unnatural control of her feelings' – spoke of trying to keep back the tears, as she and her brother went with their father to his workshop where he gave them each a pendant to take with them.

Their description of the journey into Kirkwall and then the flight south, matches exactly that of the oldest boy. Both these children left the plane at Inverness, and were taken by bus to a house where they were to meet their foster parents. They were told they would not be together, but no explanation was given. The boy was then taken to see the house where his sister would be living, before going on to his own foster home. He described is as 'quite big, with a lot of rooms' and said there would have been plenty of room for his sister there, too. For some time the separation of the two remained unexplained, until eventually he was told by his social worker that they couldn't be together in case he 'threatened' his sister so that she wouldn't tell anything she knew.

As for the little girl, she said she felt upset at not being with her brother, because there was no one else to comfort her when she was sad. She said she wasn't lonely, though, because there was an eleven-year-old girl in the house, and the family she was with looked after three babies, but they didn't have any animals in the house, and she badly missed the family pets.

Her parents said she was very quiet and not very fit when she first arrived home. She was weepy, and cried a lot at having been away for Mother's Day. She had ulcers in her mouth, and had had to eat food she was not accustomed to. This girl and her brother were Jewish, with special dietary requirements, which had been explained by the parents to the authorities, but never notified to the foster parents. The girl's mother was distressed at the state of her daughter's very long hair, and said that no one had helped her to wash and care for it all the time she'd been away; at eight years old she'd been left to cope with this fairly difficult task by herself.

As far as she could judge, said the mother, the family who had fostered her daughter had no conversation, no books, and spent their evenings watching television. They had not spent any time talking to, or trying to comfort the bewildered little girl who had arrived in their midst from Orkney.

Her son had fared rather better. Although he himself didn't feel totally comfortable with his foster family, they were kind to him, and fought on his behalf to have him sent to school. He liked that and his teacher, who listened to him talking about the situation he found himself in, and who his parents described as 'smashing'.

The boy's foster parents were generous, and very concerned about the frequent questioning sessions, which up until that point had been known as 'disclosure therapy', but suddenly the name was changed and it became 'sharing' with the children.

This boy's foster father became so concerned that he 'shared' his concerns with the Curator, the lawyer appointed by the court to represent the interests of the children. One had been appointed to each family, and the only information about the children to get back to Orkney during their five weeks away from home, came back to the family solicitors through the curators. The concern about the frequency of the children being removed to an RSSPCC Centre for questioning sessions eventually got back to Lynda Clarke, the QC for the Reporter, Gordon Sloan. In Sheriff Kelbie's findings he commended Miss Clarke for advising that this should stop, but he also cited these actions as an example of failure to regard the children as people with rights.

The boy wanted to talk to reporters, he said, because what had happened wasn't right. It wasn't nice for children to be questioned and questioned. He said the people who had interviewed him had talked about a place where children were being hurt. Some children had apparently said it was a field, and some that it was a quarry. He told them he didn't know what they were talking about, or the place they meant.

This sensitive twelve-year-old continued: 'They went on about children dressing up and about taking children into a circle where everyone was watching them and hurting them.'

The boy told them nothing like that had ever happened to him, but they persisted: 'Well, we know you saw something. It might not have happened to you, and your parents might not have done anything, but we know you saw something.'

The suggestions that his parents had hurt their children really upset him, and he told the social workers that he knew that his parents would never hurt anyone, but, he said, they thought something did happen and that's why they thought I had to go into care.

This had made him very angry. 'I did sometimes shout, and at one point they sniggered at me,' he said, 'when I said my Mum and Dad wouldn't ever do anything like that.'

The medical examination was also a matter for distress. 'I had to take off all my clothes to see if I had been hurt in any way' he said. He was angry, too, over letters he had written to his sister and to his parents. He was assured by the social worker who collected him for each session that the letters had 'got through'. The letters were never received, and he said the thing that had made him most cross was being lied to about them. He was also told he'd be getting letters from his parents, but none arrived until the day he went home. Of the whole affair, this emotional and deep-thinking boy said this should never happen to other children in the way it had happened to them, but he remained aware that some children were in a difficult situation. 'If they've got a proper reason and if children have been really hurt by their parents, then it could happen,' he said, 'but not to people that haven't been hurt and who are happy at home.'

The religious rights of the two Jewish children were at last recognised. Their parents had frequently asked that they be allowed to see a rabbi, with no success. Eventually, after a minister visited the boy, a rabbi drove from Glasgow, to where the children were staying in Invergordon, to read them the story of the Passover. But even the rabbi had to have a social worker with him all the time.

The T parents said their children seemed fine on the surface when they returned home. They were so happy to be back, and had been delighted with the bagpipe welcome at the airport and that so many of their friends had turned out to greet them, but it was a particularly bad time for such a thing to happen to a child just entering puberty, and there was a fight or a major crisis every two or three days with their son, as he tried to readjust. Their own readjustment was just as hard, they thought. Take the simple matter of getting the children up in time for school, said their father. Once it had been so natural, a romp, as they playfully pulled them from their beds in the mornings, but after the trauma they had all been through, such spontaneity had gone, and they watched their children very carefully.

Mr T didn't think they should have to explain, or apologise for, the way in which they lived their lives. They had no television in the house, for example, but many hundreds of books instead; they spent time in conversation, and were therefore, he thought, regarded as 'unusual'.

By June 1991 they had been given back a number of the items taken from their home; items such as Nepalese sculpture, a Halloween mask, a monkey mask made for a school play, and several limericks. Still missing were a lot of photographs and rolls of film. Mrs T said the roles had reversed somewhat since the children had returned home – now they comforted her as the enormity of what had happened came over her in waves. She slept badly, and her anger was constantly fuelled by the remarks of people who persistently said: 'if you knew what *we* know . . . '

The H children, a boy of nine and his eight-year-old sister, weren't quite so ready to talk to reporters. Their mother, though, outlined what she'd been able to glean from them. In this family, she had a double weight of responsibility and worry, as her husband had a serious and life-threatening illness, and suffered from epileptic attacks. His health had deteriorated rapidly throughout the whole painful time of being separated from his children.

Mrs H said it had taken its toll of both of them, as well as of the children. Her son, she said, had 'bounced back a treat'. After the euphoria of the homecoming, he had been totally hostile to his sister for a couple of weeks. He'd been exasperated and frustrated with everything and everyone, but then had reverted to his happy-go-lucky self, although he was unwilling to talk about what had happened to him. He was particularly reluctant to talk about his medical examination, but his mother thought this was perfectly natural for him, as he normally refused to acknowledge the bad things in his life, preferring to forget them.

Mrs H had nothing but praise for the family who had looked after him. They'd had two children of their own, one the same age as her son, the other three years younger, and the family had welcomed him as one of them. They cared deeply about their task of fostering, and took him out and bought him things so he'd be the same as their own children – he had, after all, arrived from Orkney with nothing at all. They enrolled him in school at once, and kindly introduced him to people as 'their nephew', explaining that his mum was in hospital. The grandfather had even got him a bike, so he wouldn't be left out.

The situation for the eight-year-old girl was very different. Her mother told how she was fostered with an elderly widow, who worked part-time, and for the first three weeks, the child had to go to the office with her, and on her return she complained that she hadn't had proper meals.

The little girl was indignant that her foster-mother had insisted on bathing her, which she could do herself, and she was very unhappy. She didn't go to school at all for the first three weeks, and then went to two different schools in the final two weeks. Mrs H was so upset by the whole story that she wrote a formal letter of complaint against the foster-mother to the Social Work Department. She said that with the money paid to foster-parents to care for children, the least she could have done was feed the child properly.

On her return home the little girl regressed almost to babyhood, according to her mother. She became very temperamental, throwing tantrums, and saying dreadful things to everyone, lashing out to hurt back as she'd been hurt. Her mother described the questioning she'd had to endure as endless. They had apparently always asked the same questions, and the child had told her that the people asking the questions hadn't listened to the answers. At one session, she had been told to draw a picture of a circle with her family in it. There had to be a man in the middle, and she had to add herself and her best friend. This was later to be described as a picture of a ritual. The child talked freely about her experiences to her mother. She was very distressed about the medical examination, and her mother thought it would take a long time for the scars to heal.

Mrs H said that the social worker responsible for her two children had read out the grounds of referral to them before the Children's Hearing took place in Orkney. There had been no explanation given at all, but the grounds had been read out to the two confused and frightened children.

Looking at her own children's experiences, and after talking to the other parents, Mrs H said the three youngest children, all aged eight, had appeared to be given the toughest time while away from their families and the safe familiarity of their homes. They'd had what she described as 'the lousy foster-parents', and their questioning had been gruelling. She wondered if this was because those asking the questions believed the youngest children would be the easiest to break down.

One of the three B children came into this category. An eight-year-old boy, who had been physically torn from his mother's arms by the police that cold February morning, he too had a hard time while he was away. He and his two elder sisters were all flown to Glasgow, and their medical examinations took place as soon as they arrived. The two sisters, unusually in this case, were allowed to stay together in the same foster home. Later the question of separating them was considered, as it was said that the elder girl was 'closing down' the younger. But the older girl knew what to do if her sister suffered an asthma attack, and was just looking after her, she told her mother after they returned home.

Their small brother, however, was sent to a different foster-family, and they were not allowed to see him. One day, when both families were at the RSSPCC centre at Strathaven where they were taken for questioning, the girls saw their brother, but even then, contact was not allowed. The girls were locked into a room with a social worker so that he would not see them: they couldn't even give him a hug to show he hadn't been forgotten. The older girl in particular was very upset at such cruelty. The little boy was very distressed that he hadn't heard a word from his mother, and when he finally got home asked her over and over again why she hadn't written to him. He was fretful and disturbed at first, and it was ten to eleven months before he began to play with his toys again and settle properly back into the routine of home. It also took a lot of tender loving care before he was able to trust people again.

He was particularly frightened about going back to school in St Margaret's Hope, the school from where he'd seen other children removed only a few months before. Now it had happened to him, and presumably it could happen again. His family couldn't reassure him as they could get no assurances themselves that children would never again be taken from school.

The families arranged a meeting with the Director of Social Work, Paul Lee. They wanted him to give such an assurance about not removing children from the islands' schools, because, they argued, schools should be places of safety themselves, and children shouldn't be frightened of going there. They warned Mr Lee that school phobia was a very real possibility. He would not give them any confirmation that this would not happen again, and they were all left with a feeling of desperate insecurity.

The two sisters came back to Orkney with many, many clothes. Their mother said their foster-family had 'spoilt them with clothes'. When they'd left, taking nothing at all with them, she had said she wanted them back with nothing but the clothes they'd gone in, and when they arrived back with bags full of clothes they'd been allowed to buy, her first inclination was to parcel them up and take them back to the Social Work Department. That would then, she thought, be an end of it all; but the girls were so excited about them, and thought of the clothes as their own so she asked them if they wanted to take them back, and in the end she didn't, she said, have the heart to do it, and so let them keep their new clothes.

Like the other children, they were delighted to be home. They enjoyed the warmth of the community and the welcome from their friends. After a few days they began looking forward again, making plans with their friends. Mrs B hoped they would go on looking forward, and she worried about the time they would stop and look back, and wonder what all this had been about, and why these things had happened to them.

Contrary to what Mrs B had been told by the Children's Panel, neither of her two daughters received any schooling during the five weeks they were away. Like the other parents, she received little or no information about them, only being told, on enquiry to Orkney's Social Work Department, that they were 'fine'. The only communication she did have was about her small son, who required dental treatment, as he had before he was taken away. She was asked to give her permission for an anaesthetic, so he could have some teeth removed. She didn't give permission, preferring to wait until the child came home, and could go to his own dentist.

This was a mother, not of three, but of six children. Three were grown up and away from home; the other three were taken from their home on 27 February, and for five weeks made to live amongst strangers, with no contact at all with their family. Mrs B had to cope with much of the trauma alone, as her husband was away working in England, and although he returned as often as he could within that troubled time, he couldn't risk losing the job that supported his family in what had been their island paradise.

Like the other parents involved, Mrs B sought answers to her questions about the conditions in which her children had been kept while they were away; like the others, she received none. There were no answers for any of the parents or their children as to why they had been taken away; why they had been allowed no contact with anyone loved or familiar; why they had been sent to the places they were, and why they had not been allowed to receive the hundreds of letters and cards sent to them by complete strangers.

Some small measure of comfort was apparently allowed eventually. The parents were permitted to take treasured cuddly toys to the Social Work Department to be forwarded to their children. These were never received, and it was some considerable time after the children's return that the toys were returned. At least one of them had very obviously been cut open, and stitched up again with a different coloured thread. 'What on earth were they looking for?' asked the perplexed father, questioning the evangelical fervour with which 'evidence' was sought, even in the toys of innocent children. Four cuddly toys were sent for her children by Mrs B, one an old and much-loved teddy. None of these toys has been returned to the family.

CHAPTER THIRTEEN

The Reporter Appeals to Court of Session

The return home of the nine children was not, of course, the end of the matter. Despite the celebrations, and the joy of their home-coming, there were matters outstanding and causing concern. The Place of Safety orders were still in force and the parents expressed fears that the Reporter, Gordon Sloan, could simply start the whole process again, uplifting the children and removing them from Orkney.

Meanwhile police enquiries had continued. A report on the allegations of ritual child abuse in Orkney had been delivered to the Crown Office in Edinburgh on 15 March, after consideration by the Procurator Fiscal acting at the time for Orkney. On 1 May the Crown Office issued a statement to say that no one was being charged with any offence, and there was no continuing criminal investigation in relation to the nine children from South Ronaldsay who had been taken from their homes on 27 February. The statement added that no further or fresh enquiries were contemplated.

The four families greeted the news with delight. It was, they believed, another step forward in their campaign to clear their names. It also made them feel that their children were a little more secure in their homes. The Crown Office decision should have meant that all the objects removed from the family homes when they were searched by police, were returned. It was many months before they were.

Gordon Sloan, the interim Reporter, as expected, appealed against Sheriff Kelbie's judgement. On 15 April it was confirmed by Strathclyde's Reporter, Fred Kennedy, that Mr Sloan had lodged an appeal in the form of an application for a stated case. This meant that Sheriff Kelbie had to submit written reasons for his judgement within fourteen days. Mr Kennedy, who was responsible for sending Gordon Sloan to Orkney, refused to comment further, saying that the proper forum for discussion of the appeal was the Court of Session and not the media.

The parents, who were relieved to have their children back, but frustrated that their cases had not been heard, generally welcomed the appeal. They said it was essential that all the evidence was heard. The decision to appeal was welcomed, too, by the RSSPCC, whose staff had been severely criticised by Sheriff Kelbie for the way they had carried out the interviews with the children.

Sheriff Kelbie's judgement was attacked from all sides. The RSSPCC said he had set back the cause of abused children for years. They wouldn't, argued the Society, come forward and tell of abuse if they thought they weren't going to be listened to. Social workers from many parts of the country voiced the same fears. After this, how could they ever persuade children to come and talk openly or allege abuse by their parents again. Nobody seemed to remember that the nine children taken from their homes on 27 February had not gone forward to tell of anything. They had not made complaints against their parents, or anyone else, and on their return home, the children who were interviewed by reporters complained bitterly that none of the interviewing social workers would believe their denials.

The Association for Reporters to Childrens Panels defended the actions of Gordon Sloan. Alan Miller, Association Secretary, passionately defended the Children's Hearing system, twenty years old in 1991. He said the apparent public criticism of the interim Reporter seemed to be based on an interpretation of the law which would now be tested by the Court of Session, and he, too, attacked Sheriff Kelbie's judgement. He criticised the Sheriff for dismissing the proceedings because the children had not been present at the first Hearings. This, said Mr Miller, brought into question a procedure which had operated sensitively and without legal challenge for many years and through many very difficult cases.

On 21 May the date for the appeal at the Court of Session in Edinburgh was set for 3 June. The court took the exceptional step of sitting on a Monday. Normally the Court of Session sits from Tuesday to Friday, but Lord Hope, the Lord President, Scotland's most senior judge, aimed to complete the appeal within a week. Sitting in Number 1 Court in Edinburgh's Parliament House with Lord Hope were Lords Allanbridge and Mayfield, and in the court were fourteen counsel representing the parents, the children and the Reporter, Gordon Sloan.

Mr Sloan himself was sitting on the public benches behind one of the Orkney mothers whose children had been removed on 27 February. With her were the two eldest of the nine children, they were there because they wanted to be; they believed they had a right to hear the appeal against the Sheriff who had ended their traumatic separation from their homes and families. They were two mature teenagers who had done a lot of growing up in a very short time. With a quiet dignity they silently represented the other children. Television crews were outside the court building, and many reporters filled the benches inside. This was the next chapter in a story that still had a long way to run.

Those reporters were to hear Mr Sloan's Counsel, Lynda Clark QC, say that their presence in the Kirkwall Court at the Proof Hearing had breached the privacy of the chamber, and that this had caused substantial and overwhelming prejudice to the proceedings. Ms Clark told the court she had five grounds of appeal against Sheriff Kelbie's decision to dismiss the Proof Hearing. She claimed he had exceeded his powers by allowing the press to attend, and that he had also delivered his decision verbally and later issued details of it to the press. The other grounds centred round his entitlement to dismiss the proceedings as incompetent, when no evidence had been led. She strongly contended that he had no legal authority to act in the way he did, particularly to comment on the tapes and transcripts of the children's interviews. He had, she said, prejudged the case in a way it was impossible to understand, and plunged the case into a procedural morass. He had taken this action, she maintained, because he did not have the power at the Proof Hearing to discharge the warrants that held the children in Places of Safety. What was open to him, she said, was to dismiss the Reporter's application, or to send the case back to the Children's Panel for review.

In his stated case to the Court of Session Sheriff Kelbie had accepted that it was not part of his duty to comment on the merits of a case before hearing the evidence, but he added: 'The only excuse I have to offer is that by that stage in the case I had seen enough to leave me in no doubt that the interests of justice, and the welfare of the children, required them to be returned to their parents as soon as possible. Nothing has since caused me to change my mind.'

In his stated case Sheriff Kelbie also said that in the welter of publicity following his ruling, there had been some misinterpretation of what he had said, and this had not been properly understood.

On the second day of the appeal, in the closing stages of her argument, Ms Clark told the court that the media publicity surrounding the case was prejudiced to such an incalculable extent that the case was being abandoned by the Reporter to the Children's Panel. She told the three judges that even if the Reporter's appeal was successful, he could not proceed further because of the damage caused by all the press and media reports.

It would, she said, be almost impossible to find witnesses whose views had not been affected by the widespread media coverage and involvement. This coverage had included Sheriff Kelbie's views, which he was not entitled to express, and interviews with potential witnesses, including child witnesses, so it was with great reluctance she had advised Mr Sloan not to proceed further. She added that the Sheriff had disqualified himself from further hearing the case, but that the appeal was continuing because the judgement could not be allowed to stand unchallenged in law. The damage he had done, she maintained, was very grave, and the press and media had treated his views as if they were views about evidence.

Ms Clark also revealed that the families had been told on 12 April that the Reporter would be abandoning the case, but he had asked for the information to be kept confidential.

In the days that followed, QCs for the families addressed the court. Mr Colin McEachran told the three senior judges that Sheriff Kelbie had relied on his conscience rather than his law books, but he also said that as the press were entitled by law to be present at Children's Hearings, it followed that if the case went to a Sheriff following a Hearing, they were also entitled to be present then. In any case journalists were under reporting restrictions which forbade them to identify the children involved. Referring to the Social Work (Scotland) Act, Mr McEachran said the press were entitled to be present 'as of right' at procedures before a Sheriff. They were also entitled to report his judgement whether they heard it for themselves in court, or read his ruling later. It was, said the QC, a public document, and he quoted a book on sheriff court procedures which stated that 'the court must administer justice in public'.

Mr Donald Robertson, QC for another family, agreed with Sheriff Kelbie about the illegality of a meeting of the Orkney Children's Panel on 1 March when a decision was taken not to bring the children back for the Hearing four days later. The counsel said no notification of the Hearing had been given to the children he represented, one of which was the eldest of the nine, the fifteen-year-old boy. Mr

Robertson also told the court that when the Curator appointed to look after the interests of the children had first gone to see this boy and his eleven-year-old brother, about a month after their removal from Orkney, he discovered they had been told nothing either in writing or verbally about the grounds of referral. They had, he said, been kept in total ignorance. After an explanation from their Curator, both boys had said very positively that they would have wanted to be present at the Children's Hearing on 5 March. This belied the impression given by the Panel that the children could not understand the allegations being made, but Mr Robertson questioned how it could seriously be suggested that a child of fifteen, or eleven, or even younger, would not be able to understand the allegations.

That, he said, was why Sheriff Kelbie had taken the view that the Children's Hearing procedure had been incompetent in law.

Mr Robertson continued: 'There is a lot of talk in the legislation about the voice of the child being heard. In this case they were not allowed to speak. The position here was that the voice of these children was not heard, and under the Act, it should have been.' The provisions of the Act, he said, gave individual rights to children, allowing them to be present at a Hearing and answer allegations made about them. They had a right to share their views and have discussions, but Orkney Children's Panel had denied that right to these children.

These were, said Mr Robertson, vitally important rights, particularly for a young person whose liberty and welfare was at stake – the liberty to live with his own family. These, he added, were not trivial matters at all, and it had to be remembered that one particular function of the Act – as well as protecting children from harm – was State interference in family relationships, giving draconian powers to remove children from their family.

Mr Gordon Jackson QC, dismissed the claim that Sheriff David Kelbie's actions had caused the Reporter to drop the proceedings. It was, he told the appeal judges, incomprehensible that in any case where the Reporter had clear evidence of child abuse by a parent that the child in question should be immediately returned to that parent because a Sheriff issued a judgement that was believed to be wrong. What the Reporter appeared to be saying, said Mr Jackson, was 'I have a perfectly good case, but I have to stop it because the Sheriff prejudiced the proceedings.' This, said the QC, left a slur hanging over the heads of the parents he represented.

Mr Robertson said the children of the family he represented had never at any time seen anyone connected with the Children's Hearing, nor had they received any document to explain what was happening to them and why. He strongly criticised the denial of the children's rights to hear and be heard, and he refuted the Reporter's contention that the proceedings were too prejudiced by Sheriff Kelbie's action to allow them to continue.

'If you are in a position where you think you have strong evidence, you should not be discouraged by anything said by a judge' he said, 'and if the Reporter's position the day before the Sheriff's decision was that these children were in such danger that they had to be kept in Places of Safety, what had changed in relation to that, if he had evidence? What changed overnight?'

QC for another family Mr Edward Targowski, the same counsel who had travelled to Orkney under difficult conditions to attend the first Children's Hearing on 5 March, said his clients' wishes had been, firstly, to have their children returned, and then to have evidence heard in the case. Because of the Reporter's action in abandoning the case, he said, there could now be no proof heard, and his statement that the publicity had grossly affected the case could only be described as 'transparent'.

On Wednesday 12 June, five days after the appeal ended, Lord President Hope delivered the judgement of the Court of Session, and in it Sheriff David Kelbie was severely criticised. The effect of what he did, the judgement concluded, was incalculable, and there was no doubt he had disqualified himself from taking any further part in the proceedings. In the opinion of the three senior judges, Sheriff Kelbie was not entitled to dismiss the application for proof as incompetent. They found that although the children had not been present at the Hearings, the case would have proceeded in exactly the same manner if they had been, as the parents had all refused to accept the grounds for referral. Whether the children had accepted the grounds or not, would simply, the judges found, have confirmed the necessity for the case to go to the Sheriff.

Although the Reporter, therefore, succeeded in the appeal, on one point the judgement did criticise his action. The paperwork in the case, it stated, left a great deal to be desired. Referring to the Children's Hearing decision on 5 March that the cases were to go to proof, the judges pointed out that no reasons were given to explain the basis upon which this decision was taken in the absence of the children. The forms submitted to apply for the Proof Hearing asserted falsely that the Children's Hearing was satisfied that the children did not understand the explanation of the grounds of referral. Sheriff Kelbie was right to point out that, as none of the children was present at the Hearing, the forms contained a statement which could not be correct. The judges said, however, that the Sheriff reached the wrong conclusion about the need for the children to be present at the hearing.

On the issue of Sheriff Kelbie's decision to allow journalists into the Sheriff Court, Lord Hope stated that as a general rule the proceedings of a court are open to the public, and thus to public scrutiny at all times. They pointed out that exceptions have to be made in special circumstances to allow the court to conduct its proceedings behind closed doors where the interests of justice require; but that, they said, was always the exception. It did not seem logical, the judgement continued, that representatives of newspapers or the media could attend the proceedings of a Children's Hearing, but must be excluded from the Sheriff's Chambers when he was dealing with the same matter. The judges concluded this was up to the discretion of the Sheriff, and subject to his control. He could decide who, other than those who had a duty or a right to be there, could attend, and for how long they could remain.

Lord Hope said they had no criticism to make of Sheriff Kelbie's decision to allow journalists to attend the proceedings in Kirkwall Sheriff Court on 3 and 4 April. The press had been present at the Children's Hearings, and the case had already received a great deal of publicity which was likely to continue. The judges thought he was right to admit the journalists to hear the rest of the debate and listen to his findings.

What they did criticise Sheriff Kelbie for, and very severely, was the way in which he used the productions in the case, those productions being the tapes and transcripts of the interviews with the children. The Court of Session understood that the Sheriff had been invited to listen to the tapes and read the transcripts in advance to assist the presentation of the case for the Reporter. This could save time in court later, but the rule is that no production becomes evidence until it has been agreed or spoken to by a witness in court. This meant, said Lord Hope, that a judge must guard against forming any views on the terms or content of a production until that point. The things Sheriff Kelbie said about the productions at the end of his findings, said the Court of Session judgment, made it plain that he went far beyond the legitimate exercise of preparation. He had allowed himself to form views about the content of the productions and then to express those views publicly, it was stated, which would have made it impossible for him to bring a fair and balanced judgement to the issues which were before him when evidence was being led.

They could not, said the Lord President, attribute any blame to Sheriff Kelbie for any effect which there might have been on the evidence of witnesses, as stated by Counsel for the Reporter, Lynda Clark. Equally, they couldn't excuse his conduct on the ground that the release of the children that same day showed that he was right. They couldn't accept his excuse that he was acting according to his conscience because it was his duty to conduct the proceedings within the law, and he owed that duty as much to the children and their parents as he did to the Reporter. They said, too, that those with important responsibilities under the Social Work (Scotland) Act were entitled to be heard before their actions were condemned. So Sheriff Kelbie was condemned for failing in his duty to all parties involved.

In presenting the judgement, Lord President Hope praised the 'genius' of the Children's Hearing system. He said that the misfortunes of the Orkney case should not be allowed to detract from a reform that had earned so much praise for its handling of all cases involving children.

There were many calls for action following the appeal to the Court of Session, including a thorough examination of the rights of children in disclosure interviews, the need for social workers to be much better trained in child protection, and for small Social Work Departments to have easier access to specialist advice. A broader look at access to children in care and the rights of parents was called for, and the suitability of Places of Safety.

The RSSPCC and the British Association of Social Workers welcomed the ruling from the three senior judges. They said it had clearly vindicated the actions of the Children's Panel and of the Reporter. And a brief statement came from the Chief Executive of Orkney Islands Council, Ron Gilbert. He said the Social Work Department would take cognisance of the statement from the Court of Session, and they were now looking forward to a wide-ranging judicial inquiry which he hoped would give council employees the opportunity to explain their actions and the reasons they carried them out.

The Orkney parents themselves challenged the decision of the Reporter, Gordon Sloan, not to pursue the case to enable proof to be heard in court. One father said he was not surprised at the Court of Session judgement.

'We were never in any doubt,' he said, 'that it was Sheriff David Kelbie and not the law of the land who saved our children,' and he continued, 'we will still be pushing for the case to go to a proof hearing, Mr Gordon Sloan may not be legally obliged to continue the case, but he is morally obliged. Either our children are at risk or they aren't, and it can't be left as though the case against us is still there.'

That, however, is exactly where it was left. The Reporter formally abandoned the case, and the parents were left with only the promised Inquiry to look forward to.

The Secretary of State for Scotland, Ian Lang, had announced in April that a full judicial inquiry into the events in Orkney would be held. Within three hours of Gordon Sloan's appeal to the Court of Session being upheld by Scotland's most senior judges, Mr Lang announced that the Inquiry would be led by Lord Clyde. This appointment, said the Scottish Secretary, would ensure an authoritative investigation of the issues.

CHAPTER FOURTEEN

The Inquiry Begins

On 19 June 1991 the Secretary of State for Scotland, Ian Lang, announced the terms of reference for the judicial inquiry to be conducted by Lord Clyde. The formal terms of reference were set out as follows:

'To inquire into the actings of Orkney Islands Council (in particular those of their Social Work Department and of their Reporter to the Children's Panel for their area), of the Northern Constabulary and of all persons acting on behalf of either of them, and into the effect on those actings of the attendant publicity, in relation to:

(1) The decision to seek authority to take to a place of safety nine children resident in South Ronaldsay.

(2) The removal of those children from their homes on February 27 1991.

(3) The detention of those children in places of safety following the removal and until they returned to their home (and in particular how they were cared for and interviewed while so detained).

(4) The decision not to continue proceedings before the Sheriff for a finding on the evidence.

— and to make recommendations.'

Mr Lang said the terms of reference were designed to enable Lord Clyde to carry out an authoritative investigation of the main issues involved. The Secretary of State also said that although legal aid was not available for such inquiries, he had decided that the Scottish Office should nevertheless meet the reasonable costs of legal representation of the parents whose children were removed to a Place of Safety.

That statement brought immediate relief for the families and for the South Ronaldsay Parents' Action Committee whose fund-raising efforts, while successful and continuing, would have been hard pressed to meet the full legal costs of representation for the parents during the inquiry. They all welcomed the remit set by Mr Lang, and solicitor John Moir said he thought it was sufficiently wide to deal with all the principal concerns that had arisen. He particularly welcomed the examination of the Reporter Gordon Sloan's decision not to proceed with the case. 'That decision,' said Mr Moir 'denied the parents the opportunity to have their names cleared in an appropriate forum' and he added that although the inquiry could not apportion guilt, he hoped the parent's innocence would become self-evident because of it.

Chairman of the parents' action group, Dr Helen Martini, was a little more cautious in her welcome of the remit, and called for the inquiry to discuss what was meant by the term 'ritual' which had been in the grounds of referral, and had initially been used by Gordon Sloan. The Orkney and Shetland MP Jim Wallace also welcomed the details for the inquiry and said he very much hoped that some positive recommendations to improve procedures and practice in this area of child-care would emerge. He also welcomed the Secretary of State's decision to make public funds available to the four families. He said Mr Lang had responded promptly and properly on the issue.

Orkney Islands Council issued a statement. It, too, welcomed the wide terms of reference, and expressed appreciation that the arrangements for the inquiry had been made so quickly after the Court of Session Appeal proceedings. The council believed that all the agencies involved would be able to place on record the role they had played, and their reasons for taking the course of action they had followed. It hoped too that any revision of guidelines and procedures which followed the inquiry would be suitable for the differing needs of small communities as well as for the more densely populated parts of Scotland.

Lord Clyde arrived in Orkney to hold a preliminary hearing in Kirkwall's Town Hall on 3 July. This was to establish the rules for the inquiry itself. He said then that he wanted to spare the children the ordeal of having to give evidence in public, and that he would commission an independent psychologist to interview the children and then report, as a witness, to the inquiry. 'I suspect,' he said, 'the children have probably already been subjected to quite enough questioning over the past months,' and he called for the co-operation of the parents to ensure that the children's evidence was given to the appointed expert. He said, too, that although the investigation was not concerned with other cases, if there were lessons to be learned from this one, then the benefit of those lessons could be shared.

Lord Clyde decided at the preliminary hearing which individuals and organisations should be legally represented. These included Orkney's acting interim Reporter, Gordon Sloan, Orkney Islands Council, the Director of Social Work Paul Lee, social workers involved in executing the original Place of Safety orders, the RSSPCC, Strathclyde and Highland Regions, whose social workers were also involved in the case, and the Northern Constabulary. The families were to be allowed two senior and two junior counsel between them, and Lord Clyde agreed that the minister, the Reverend Morris McKenzie, should also be legally represented.

Two expert assessors were appointed to sit with Lord Clyde during the inquiry. One was Miss Anne Black, a divisional Director of Social Work for Lothian Region, and the other Dr Hugh Morton, a consultant in child and adolescent psychiatry with Tayside Health Board. Lord Clyde said these two would advise him on certain professional aspects of the matters under examination. He announced that the inquiry would begin, in the Town Hall in Kirkwall, on 26 August.

The inquiry opened with a promise by Lord Clyde that it would be 'objective to a fault'. 'It is not,' he said, 'a litigation between opposing parties, but an objective inquiry into what has happened'. Hopes were high on all sides; the families hoping that although no evidence would be tested, the inquiry would conclude they had had no part in abusing their children, and that their children had not been subject to the abuse of which the parents stood charged. The authorities, social workers and other agencies involved in the case hoped the inquiry's findings would be favourable to them.

Lord Clyde warned the assembled press and media reporters that they must not compromise the inquiry in any way by interviewing those involved before or after they had given evidence. He stressed that there was to be no public discussion of evidence outside the inquiry and told witnesses not to comment to the press. 'This inquiry is to be held before me,' he said.

Thirteen counsel, including nine QCs, filled the benches in Kirkwall's town hall. Solicitors, journalists, the families, members of the Parents' Action Committee, and interested observers crowded in. Many of them were to remain throughout the whole of the inquiry, the journalists reporting daily to newspapers, radio and television the evidence given by the witnesses of the day, and others drawing their own conclusions about the direction the inquiry seemed to be taking. Some described it as 'a strange animal that has taken on a life of its own'.

The proceedings began by going back in time and recounting some of the history of the W family. Counsel to the inquiry, Donald MacFadyen QC, said that at least some of the aspects concerning that family needed to be examined. He said that on 6 February 1991 interviews with the W children in care by WPC Linda Williamson and RSSPCC worker Liz Maclean had begun. During these, he said, three children 'made statements understood to indicate that the children of the four families who are [the] subject of this inquiry had been involved in sexual abuse'. On 14 February, he continued, the decision to seek Place of Safety orders was taken by Orkney Islands Council's Director of Social Work, Paul Lee, the department's fieldwork team leader, Sue Millar, and two police officers, and on 26 February an application was made to the Sheriff in Kirkwall for Place of Safety orders for the nine children removed from their homes in the early morning of 27 February.

Paul Lee was the first witness. As he began to give his evidence the parents heard for the first time the detailed allegations which had led to their children being taken. They were tense and strained as they heard him recount the stories from the three W children. Interviewed separately, he said, they had each told horrific stories of bizarre sexual abuse, ritual dancing and music after dark in an Orkney quarry. He described these stories as 'identical in substance'. They referred to someone called Morris. Mr Lee later identified this person as the Reverend Morris McKenzie, minister for St Margaret's Hope and Burray. One of the three children had said: 'he makes us run into a circle and he stands in the middle,' Mr Lee told the inquiry. She had made several drawings, one with a stick-like figure with a crook coming from its arm and said: 'That's Morris in the middle'. She had described a long black cloak, a hood and a black mask which covered his eyes and said: 'he hooks you when you're dancing and pulls you towards him. He's growing a beard and he rubs on you and hurts you. We don't need to talk about the dirty stuff.' The child had then described how the hooded figure had sexual intercourse with her. She had named a number of people involved, and talked about intercourse between other adults and children. One of her sisters and a brother had, said Mr Lee, told basically the same story, naming a total of fourteen people.

'From the information given by the three W children,' he said, 'it was possible to identify people from four other families in South Ronaldsay – the M, B, H and T families,' but he admitted very little was known about them in the Social Work Department.

Mr Lee also admitted that Scottish Office guidelines had not been used in conducting this case. He said normal social work practice was inappropriate, as they suspected organised abuse on a wide scale in the island, and the guidelines didn't deal with that. They hadn't even re-read the 'Effective Intervention' document; he said, 'We were trying to put the child first – that affected the way we dealt with it.'

The suggestion for the early morning move had come, said Mr Lee, from Sam Mactaggart, Divisional Manager of the RSSPCC based in Glasgow. Mr Mactaggart was involved at all stages before, during and after the removal of the children – and Mr Mactaggart was appointed an Assistant Director of Social Work with Orkney Islands Council in April 1991. Together with Paul Lee, Sue Millar, and the police, Mr Mactaggart wanted the children separated, taking the view, said Mr Lee, that children disclose better when separated from siblings. They had agreed, too, continued the Social Work Director, not to contact the South Ronaldsay GP Dr Richard Broadhurst, doctor to all the children, because it was felt he was too involved with the W children to give an impartial view; nor did they contact the educational psychologist Peter Shearer, who'd been involved extensively with the W family because 'unsubstantiated allegations' had been made against him, said Mr Lee.

He described to the inquiry the detailed plans that were laid for the removal of the nine children. He said the Council Convener, Vice-Convener, Chairman of Social Work and Chief Executive were all informed of what was about to take place, and he told how social workers from Orkney, Strathclyde and Central Regions had carried out the morning raids on 27 February, with police from the Northern Constabulary. The police, said Mr Lee, had been instrumental in the decision to take the children in the early morning. 'They wanted to separate the parents from the children for interview,' he told the inquiry. 'They were giving us clear indications that criminal prosecutions were under contemplation.'

Mr Lee also admitted that doubts about the operation had been expressed by two of the Strathclyde social workers. They had told him that they and their colleagues had serious misgivings about the lack of information they'd been given about the children's disclosures that had led to the action being taken, but Mr Lee said they did not want 'contamination of such disclosures'. He also explained the reasoning behind the decision not to allow the children to take personal belongings. According to the RSSPCC, said Mr Lee, 'possessions from home might have possible symbolic meanings'. He said that Mrs Sue Millar, his team leader, held the same view.

He criticised the press and media coverage of the case saying that as the days progressed, the press situation became more and more difficult, and it was very hard to keep working normally. He told of reporters ringing his doorbell at eight o'clock in the morning, of a car staying outside his house all day and following his wife and daughters to Stromness. He said some of the media reporting had upset both himself and his staff, and he told the inquiry that after the removal of the children, death threats by mail and telephone had been made to his department. He denied the newspaper allegation that members of Orkney Islands social work staff had ever attended a much-publicised conference on satanic sexual abuse organised by a Christian evangelical group in Aberdeen in November 1990.

'I found this report particularly ludicrous, as in November 1990 this department was fully committed in the case of the W family,' he said.

During Paul Lee's evidence Lord Clyde halted the proceedings for three quarters of an hour to reprimand some sections of the media for their reporting of the inquiry. Complaints from all the counsel involved, including certain reports and pictures, were shown to the judge in chambers. Afterwards, without naming any publication he said: 'In some respects these reports sought to prejudge issues which are for my determination.' He was particularly concerned about the possible identification of any of the children from the reports. 'Irresponsible and sensational reporting does no service to the public and no service to this public inquiry,' he said.

Mr Lee gave evidence for ten days. During this time he was asked if the families under suspicion following the disclosures by the W children were monitored by his department. He said no, and explained that because of the confidential nature of the case and the close nature of the community, it hadn't been possible. 'Your main concern and priority was secrecy, not the protection of the children?' asked the counsel. 'I understand that that was the case,' replied the social work director.

He defended the lack of consultation with anyone in South Ronaldsay saying it was difficult to know who to trust. His department had not approached the Lord Lieutenant of Orkney, who lived there, the local councillor, two JPs resident in the island, a local care worker or even the former deputy director of social work, whose home was also there. All could have given a clear picture of life in South Ronaldsay, as could the district nurse and the local GP. 'The doctor had perhaps been aware of some issues going on in the W family but he had never communicated them to us,' said Mr Lee. And he said that some corroboration of the allegations had come from several of the nine children after they were taken into care in interviews with the RSSPCC workers. But he did not give any indication as to what the corroborating information was.

Asked to justify the decision to send the eldest of the nine children to a former List D school and not to a foster home like the rest, Mr Lee said that it was the only placement Strathclyde could offer for the boy. He admitted it was not an ideal situation, but that it was all they could arrange given the time factor. He admitted, too, that while Sue Millar had travelled to the mainland to arrange places of safety for the nine children, she had not inspected them for their suitability.

Questioned closely about the correspondence sent to and from the children and never received, Paul Lee said that Sam Mactaggart of the RSSPCC agreed with him that the children should receive no letters or cards. He couldn't explain to the inquiry why letters written to their parents by two of the children in care, on 12 March, had not been delivered until 21 May, long after they had returned home. At this point in the inquiry their mother dissolved into tears. Mr Lee said the co-ordinator of the case was Mrs Millar and the question should be taken up with her. He told counsel that no apology had ever been sent to the parents regarding the non-delivery of the letters, and admitted, on questioning, that it ought to have been.

One counsel for two of the families, on the subject of the medical examinations of the children, asked Paul Lee if he was aware that none of the parents had given their consent for the examinations. 'I cannot recall being aware of that,' he replied. The examinations, the inquiry was told, showed *no* signs of abuse. 'In view of this did you review the Place of Safety warrants?' asked Nigel Morrison QC. 'No,' answered Mr Lee, and he said it was a point of debate whether the parents should be entitled to see the results of the medical evidence.

'Do you accept that you primarily took the children into care purely so that they could be questioned?' asked Mr Morrison. 'We acted purely for the safety of the children,' replied Paul Lee. 'Did you not subject the children to system abuse?' continued the counsel. 'That may be your opinion, it is not mine,' answered the social work director.

On the eighth day of the inquiry Lord Clyde heard how the senior team leader, Sue Millar, had tendered her resignation from Orkney's Social Work Department less than three weeks before the dawn raids. In a letter read out in full she strongly criticised the way Paul Lee ran the department with regard to child-care matters. She complained that he was 'autocratic' and lacked serious commitment to her and her team and said there was a complete lack of any policy on child-care issues. In her letter, dated 8 February, she said she felt she had been forced to resign because she had been continually frustrated in her attempts to offer her professional expertise. Mr Lee had already told the inquiry that he had found the department undermanned and under-resourced when he arrived to take over in February 1990. The Department, he said, had been standing still for ten years. He was, he continued, in the middle of re-organising it, and it was inevitable that staff should be under extra pressure at such a time.

Specific details of what some of the nine children had said during interviews while they were in care were given to the inquiry by counsel for the RSSPCC Mr Hugh Campbell QC during his cross-examination of Paul Lee. One little girl had told RSSPCC worker Liz McLean that 'a bad man had hurt her', and there were stories of a circle in a field where children and parents had gone together and children had been hurt. According to notes taken by the Society's workers they talked about a man with 'a long black dress' or a 'black cloak with buttons'. The notes continued that one child had said the Reverend McKenzie had used his finger to abuse her sometimes, and there was talk of wearing turtle suits which were kept in a plastic box in Morris McKenzie's kitchen. Other notes said that one boy refused to go home the day the children were released. He said bad things happened at home, and that a named person groped at his genitals. He later retracted this.

The next witnesses were social workers employed by Orkney Islands Council. They each told of their part in the operation to take the children from their homes, and described the different reactions and emotions of the children. They spoke too about their involvement over the years with the W family. They told the inquiry that only six days before the early morning uplift, the social workers in Orkney knew practically nothing about the families or any of the children, and there were no case files.

Four of them, Mary Finn, Michelle Miller, Julie Lee and Lynn Drever, had sent a memo to the social work director, Paul Lee, and to the team leader Sue Millar on 25 March. In it they voiced their concern over the lack of information available about the progress of the case. They complained there had been no updates within the department, and outlined their own feelings of vulnerability because no arrests had been made, and no prosecutions had followed the removal of the children. They also expressed their worries over the apparent entrenchment between the Social Work Department and the Reporter to the Children's Panel over which professionals should have access to the children. There appeared to be a difference of opinion, and the social workers didn't know exactly who wanted what.

Mary Finn told the inquiry she felt there was no reason why the brother and sister with whom she had been involved should have been allowed no contact during their time in care. The boy had been particularly distressed at being separated and she had told both Liz McLean and Sue Millar that she thought they should be allowed some contact. She also told of a phone call she had had from Sue Millar to say the social workers drafted in from Strathclyde and Central Regions, to assist with the removal, were not to be allowed to see the children again. 'I think she believed that the workers were becoming emotionally involved with the children,' said Mrs Finn. A Strathclyde social worker, Rab Murphy, countermanded that instruction later in the day, she continued, and said she was to tell the social workers from outwith Orkney they could visit the children the next day. Mrs Finn also told the inquiry that the press coverage had put the children under undue stress, and she did not believe it was in their best interests.

Giving her evidence next, Michelle Miller told the inquiry that even after the children were returned to their parents she was worried about their welfare. She had, she said, dealt with the W family for years and believed the allegations made by the three children. She joined Paul Lee in criticising the conduct of the press and media, but added her condemnation of the legal profession. The press had been used, she said, to put over one side of the story and had distorted the facts, and she believed the lawyers had used jargon to overwhelm members of the Children's Panel.

Referring to the first Hearing of the panel on 5 March, Mrs Miller said that police had had to escort her and Sue Millar through a shouting, swearing mob waving placards. She told Nigel Morrison QC that they had sworn directly at her, but she was not aware of anyone being arrested for Breach of the Peace. She also defended the fact that the first Hearing had not been held the day after the children's removal. 'It would have been difficult as they were off the island,' she said. At the second Hearing, although there were fewer people present, Mrs Miller said the behaviour of the family representatives went beyond being in the best interests of the children, and she found it unacceptable. She told the counsel for Orkney Islands Council, Donald Mackay QC, that the Hearings were totally out of control.

Michelle Miller also expressed her own concerns over the Orkney Social Work Department's child-care policies. She told the inquiry that the social workers were not allowed to question Sue Millar's handling of cases, and if they did query anything, her response was a great deal of anger and a questioning of their own abilities in this field.

Other island social workers gave largely supportive evidence. They had expected police to charge parents after the removal of the children, and nothing had happened since to make them change their minds over the need for the action they had taken. Julie Lee, a newcomer to the department, said that on the face of it, it looked as if a paedophile ring was operating in South Ronaldsay. There were, she said, a number of questions in her mind about interviewing techniques, and lack of information, but she had 'accepted the professionalism' of the police, the RSSPCC, and the management of Orkney Social Work Department.

She described the final planning meeting before the February uplift of the children. It was held in a basement room, known as 'the bunker' in the council headquarters in Kirkwall, and around fifty people had crowded in. It had been confusing, and she thought it would be easy for people to misunderstand what was being explained. Julie Lee also expressed concern over the interviewing of the children by RSSPCC worker Liz McLean, saying someone new to the case might have been preferable, and that Mrs

McLean might be 'subconsciously drawing out the information she might wish'.

Charles Fraser, the social worker who was also a member of the evangelical Christian group in Orkney, said the allegations had been described to him as straightforward sexual abuse and not as the satanic or ritual practices referred to in the press and media. He believed organised abuse had been taking place, but thought that was quite distinct from ritualistic abuse. Several of the social workers said the word 'ritual' had not been used within the department. Later, while questioning Lynn Drever, QC Nigel Morrison produced a document written by WPC Linda Williamson referring to ritual sexual abuse.

When the team leader Sue Millar began to give her evidence she described herself as 'disturbed and demoralised' at the lack of child-care guidelines available in Orkney's Social Work Department when she arrived there to take up her appointment on 1 July 1990. She said the team were not used to being managed, and said she felt uncomfortable with no written procedures to follow, especially in view of the department's involvement with the W family. She described the way in which the department had dealt with the W children and the events leading up to their removal into care in November 1990.

She told the inquiry how she had heard from Liz McLean of the disclosures being made by three members of the W family on 13 February. One child, she said, had made it clear that she had been abused by the Reverend McKenzie, and that this was penetrative sexual abuse. The child had referred to the minister as 'The Master' said Mrs Millar. She described how the nine children who were removed on 27 February had been mentioned as further details of the disclosures emerged. It was obvious, she said, that the parents of these children were also involved. The co-operation between her department, the RSSPCC and the police got under way. The police wanted to remove the adults at the same time as the children, and to question the children at once, but Sue Millar said she felt this would be too upsetting for the children.

Sue Millar's evidence matched that of her colleagues, and she condemned the action of Sheriff Kelbie in dismissing the Proof Hearing. His remarks, she said, had caused 'incalculable damage' and had 'incited a hostile mob to storm the office of Orkney Islands Social Work Department, trapping herself and colleagues in the building'. She told the inquiry that she strongly disagreed with the decision to let the children return to their own homes from their foster homes on the mainland, and had urged that fresh Place of Safety orders should be obtained. The interim Reporter to the Children's Panel, Gordon Sloan, had, however, refused to follow this course of action, she said.

She also described the pressure affecting the director, Paul Lee. She said he'd been unable to cope, and was unable to defend himself against the press and 'screaming families'. He had, she continued, 'struggled to keep his thoughts under control under the pressure of an aggressive and biased media campaign'. Mr Lee, she said, was upset and worn out.

Sue Millar said she had contacted the director of the RSSPCC Raymond Starrs, to voice her concerns about Mr Lee, and to discuss ways of easing the pressure on him, and of handling the enormous press demands.

She was asked by QC Edward Targowski, acting for the parents, if she had told one set of parents that she would be happy to talk to them about their relationships with their children, and that she'd said: 'Remember an abused child will never fully recover until an abuser admits his guilt'. She denied saying that, but said that the department would be happy to work with parents on these matters, even if the things the police had talked about had happened. She also denied that she had offered parents a deal if they admitted they had taken part in the alleged abuse.

Counsel for the Orkney and Strathclyde field social workers, Mr James Taylor asked Mrs Millar to recall a conversation that took place in a corridor in the Social Work Department on 8 February, nineteen days before the removal of the children. She was quoted as saying that 'she had enough evidence to sink the *Titanic*', but she replied she had no memory of that conversation.

Under cross-examination by Mr Targowski, Sue Millar said she had felt very uneasy about the lack of support offered to the parents after the removal of the children. She said Orkney just did not have the resources to cover all aspects of the operation, and so they had concentrated on the welfare of the children. In any event, she said, she was not very sure about the reaction they would have got from the parents if they had been able to offer support. Their attitude towards her had been hostile, and she was surprised that the anger and concern of the four families should have lasted so long. When they came to the Social Work Department, she said, they were willing to speak to her colleagues, but not to her. She also said that because of their hostility, they were excluded from important case conferences held to discuss the welfare of their children. As the chairperson, she told Mr Targowski, she had a duty to see that the meetings were non-disruptive. 'I think your clients have to take some responsibility in terms of the hostility which they generated to the extent that we had to take this very unusual decision,' she told the QC. Two case conferences were held, one while the children were still in care, and the other five days after their return on 9 April. At this time each family was allocated a social worker.

Mrs Millar said the media involvement made it very difficult for the social workers to work with the parents. They had become unreachable because of their 'aggressive stance' she told the inquiry. 'The Hearing System could have dealt appropriately with this case had it not been abandoned,' she said. 'It is my wish that the Place of Safety orders be renewed.'

A social worker from Central Region, Frances Connor, described how she and colleagues from Central and Strathclyde Regions were frustrated at the lack of information they received from Orkney social workers. She said too that they didn't feel enough thought had gone into what was to happen to the nine children after they were taken into care. She told Lord Clyde they had been very close to pulling out the night before the removal, but had been told that the operation would go ahead with or without them, so they had decided to take part. They had to accept that Orkney Islands Council was confident it had enough evidence, she said. Lord Clyde asked her for her assessment of the operation, and she replied that she and the other workers from mainland Scotland felt it could have been done differently, and that the best interests of the children were not always considered. She added, however, that there was reason to believe the children had been abused, and it was correct to remove them from their homes.

Senior Strathclyde social worker Rab Murphy said he had been led to believe that the police had enough evidence to arrest all the adults named in the alleged sex ring, but at the briefing meeting the night before the children were removed, he heard a senior Orkney policeman say: 'Without hard evidence we have nothing,' and he had added: 'If we have nothing else, then the statements the children have made are worthless.' Mr Murphy also described the barrier that had developed between the outside social workers and the Orkney social work management almost as soon as they arrived in the island. Another senior social worker from Strathclyde, Sandy Fraser, told the inquiry he regretted that he and his colleagues ever took part in the Orkney dawn raids on the limited information they were given.

Maureen Hughes, also a senior Strathclyde social worker said she had very little confidence in the RSSPCC worker who had obtained the disclosures from the W children. Maureen Hughes told the inquiry she'd asked Liz McLean a number of questions to 'assess her credibility', but she'd been dissatisfied with the response. She said Mrs McLean's answers to questions about techniques and methodology had been vague and unsatisfactory. She said she was also concerned that the three W children, who had been in care since the previous November, had all given their disclosures in the same week. 'I thought that was quite a coincidence,' she said. 'Children normally disclose at their own pace and I was quite suspicious of the fact that they had disclosed to the same person'. Mrs Hughes also told the inquiry that the working relationship between Liz McLean and Sue Millar was one where they 'fed off each other', which was not a helpful situation.

She was critical, too, of the early morning raids to take children into care, and said they almost smacked of 'Gestapo tactics', and she said that RSSPCC workers who were brought in to help when the children were removed were totally inexperienced and 'immobilised by fear'.

The children who were taken to the Camoran Children's Centre in Kirkwall prior to their flight out of Orkney, were adamant that no one had hurt them. A twelve-year-old boy said nothing at all had happened to him or to his sister, and that their mum and dad had done nothing to hurt them. This was the evidence given to the inquiry by a member of the Camoran staff, Michael Thorpe. It was corroborated by the officer in charge of Camoran, Ann Donnan. She described how distraught a thirteen-year-old girl had been, and how her eleven-year-old sister had said no one had hurt her, although she did admit to being bullied at school.

The headmaster of Geilsland school in Ayrshire, where the fifteen-year-old boy was sent, said he had questioned the need for such a placement when he heard the boy was to be sent to his school. Ranald Mair said it had been decided to put the boy in a residential school as he was expected to react badly to being taken into care. He said he was also told there was uncertainty over whether the boy was a perpetrator or a victim of the alleged abuse. Mr Mair also told the inquiry that he had made sure the boy had access to the television reports of the case, and all the daily newspapers.

At the end of the first month of the inquiry the families at the centre of the South Ronaldsay alleged abuse case invited Lord Clyde to visit their homes in Orkney's southernmost island. On 14 November he took up the invitation, but with the intention of getting more idea of the location of the houses, and to find out the exact position of the rooms, rather than holding conversations with the families. At the same time the slow progress of the inquiry was criticised by Orkney Islands Council. All the precognitions had not been gathered before the inquiry began, and councillors said the delays were a matter of considerable concern. Nor, they believed, was the pace of the inquiry in the interests of the council staff, the families involved or the community.

Money was becoming a problem, too. The RSSPCC appealed to Orkney Islands Council to defray their costs during the inquiry, which were rising steeply, and which the charity could not afford. Orkney Islands Council expressed sympathy, but said they could not afford it either, and eventually the Scottish Office stepped in with cash aid to help with the Society's legal costs.

More financial problems caused by the inquiry were to hit the headlines. Early in November, the funding Paul Lee had been receiving from the British Association for Social Workers for his legal costs, ran out. They had exhausted their legal budget for the whole of the UK on Mr Lee's case. An urgent approach was made to the Scottish Office, but no government help was made available to Mr Lee, although by this time the Secretary of State Ian Lang had agreed to meet much of the legal costs of the four families, the Reverend Morris McKenzie, the former social work team leader Sue Millar, and the RSSPCC. Mr Lee said his position at the inquiry was untenable and he and his lawyers walked out. A Scottish Office spokesman said that the Secretary of State did not feel it would be proper for him to fund the representation at a public inquiry of a serving official of a local authority. The responsibility for that rested with either the authority or with the individual's professional association. Isles MP Jim Wallace wrote to the Secretary of State and asked him to reconsider his decision.

CHAPTER FIFTEEN

The Inquiry Continues

The cost of the inquiry dominated most of November. By this stage it was already estimated at over £2 million, and Orkney Islands Council was seriously considering withdrawing altogether. As well as its own legal representation, the council was funding that of the interim Reporter to the Children's Panel, Gordon Sloan. Strathclyde Region, whose social workers had assisted in the early morning uplift of the children in February, were also worried about their share of the costs, and were threatening to pull out as well. Councillor Charles Gray, the leader of Strathclyde, said his council had written a strongly worded letter to Orkney asking them to meet their obligation to his region. He added: 'There is a danger that we are losing sight of the real reason for the inquiry, the welfare of innocent children.' With huge bills to come from Highland Region and the Northern Constabulary, Orkney planned to send a delegation of councillors and officials to meet Scottish Office Minister Michael Forsyth, and plead their case for funding.

The council were annoyed by the attitude of the Scottish Office, believing the inquiry should be funded sufficiently by the government to allow it to proceed meaningfully. The government attitude was that as the inquiry was looking at the actions of Orkney's Social Work Department, then the council must pay its share. Councillors were worried that the cost of the whole thing could add £150 to the poll tax.

The delegation, which included Council Convener Jackie Tait, Chief Executive Ron Gilbert, and the Chairman of the Social Work Committee, Mrs Mairhi Trickett, flew to London to plead for financial support, and they won the day. Michael Forsyth promised that more government money would be made available to defray the rapidly rising costs of the inquiry, and said that poll tax payers would not have to foot the bill. The agreement was worked out on similar lines to those applied when the government assisted the Cleveland inquiry. It was also agreed that the council would fund Paul Lee's representation, which would also be assisted by the Scottish Office.

Lord Clyde himself went to the Scottish Office to express his own concerns. He met with the Solicitor General and other representatives because of the possibility of certain parties pulling out of the inquiry for financial reasons. When the inquiry resumed, he told those gathered in Kirkwall Town Hall that although this was a local inquiry, at the end its relevance might well be found to spread far beyond Orkney. He said the next two stages of the inquiry involved the evidence of the police and the four families, and he hoped that would be finished before Christmas.

The first police witness was Detective Superintendent George Gough from the Northern Constabulary. He told the inquiry that the intense and sensational publicity following the removal of the nine children from their homes hampered police enquiries. The publicity, he said, had undoubtedly influenced public opinion in favour of the families, and to the detriment of the ongoing police investigation. He said he was convinced by the disclosures of the W children and their accompanying drawings, that the stories of organised child sex abuse were credible.

His strong criticism of the press and media coverage was echoed by his colleague, Detective Inspector James Heddle. He told the inquiry he felt he and his officers were unable to search for the quarry that had been mentioned in the disclosures, because of the press activity on South Ronaldsay. He also said that four of the nine children had backed up the sex abuse claims so convincingly that it was felt they should remain in care. He said an eight-year-old girl had described a man in a black cloak dancing in a ring and hooking children into the circle with a stick. He added that the child was embarrassed when she talked about this.

Then it was the parents' turn to have their say. Seven of the eight parents spent some time giving evidence, but some of them said afterwards they felt they had been effectively gagged. The social workers, they said, had been allowed free rein to name names, and allege all sorts of behaviour on the part of the parents. They themselves, they said, were interrupted and stopped from giving evidence if it became 'too personalised'. Their full precognitions, they said, were not used, and much of what they had written in them was paraphrased with huge chunks left out. When they had prepared their precognitions, they had been told by the lawyers that these would be used as a starting point, and expanded upon. This, they said, did not happen.

Some of the parents, however, were full of praise for the process
of law as they witnessed it during the inquiry. They had great respect
for Lord Clyde and his handling of it, although others felt he did
not stop certain lines of questioning often enough. Nor, they said,
did he make the Reporter, Gordon Sloan, produce notes he had in
his possession about his meetings with his QC Lynda Clark over the
abandonment of the case against them.

Each of the parents, in turn, told the inquiry what had happened at
7 o'clock on 27 February, when police and social workers had arrived
at their homes to remove their children. Mr M, giving his evidence,
was shown the pen-portrait of one of his sons prepared by the primary
school head teacher on South Ronaldsay, Doreen McLeman. 'If this
is what Miss McLeman has given as a pen-portrait of my child I
think the parents of South Ronaldsay will be very unhappy with
her as a head teacher,' he said. This remark was greeted with an
outburst of clapping from several members of the public. They
were rebuked by Lord Clyde, who told them they had to behave
responsibly while they were at the inquiry.

Mr M was told he he should not be protesting his innocence while
in the witness box. The question of whether sex abuse was or was
not happening was not within the remit of the inquiry, and Mr M's
denials could not, therefore, be challenged under cross-examination.
'Unfortunately,' said the father, 'after three months of listening to
slurs and innuendos it is difficult not to redress the balance'.

Asked about the press and media campaign in favour of the
families, Mr M denied that they had managed to organise this.
He said the journalists had gone to the first public meeting in St
Margaret's Hope expecting to hear 'a dirty vicar story', but by the
end of the evening they had seemed to realise that here was real
injustice.

Mrs M said the press and media had treated them with respect and
sympathy, and she praised the way the story had been covered. 'We
were in a state of shock and gave them our souls,' she said. She told
the inquiry that she hadn't been surprised by the raid because of her
family's involvement with the W family, who lived quite close to their
South Ronaldsay farm. She said the removal of her children, along
with the seven others that morning, had created a climate of fear in
the island. Other people were making contingency plans to protect
their own children, she said. Some had armed themselves with guns,
and there were plans to light flares to warn others; one family had

even built a secret hiding place under the floorboards where they could conceal their children if necessary. It was a very frightening situation, she said, with many parents questioning whether their children would be taken next.

She described, too, her own personal fears about her children, while they were in care. She told of the panic attacks she had experienced at bedtime each night, when the plight of her sons, particularly the older one, led her, she said 'to the brink of madness'. She had needed immediate reassurance from the authorities that her children were all right, she said, but had been unable to get it.

Mrs B broke down as she gave her evidence. She said the social workers responsible for the children's welfare while in care were 'sick', and said her eight-year-old son had come home 'a very disturbed, sad little boy, with stress written all over his face'. He had, she said, been through five weeks of hell. QC for the RSSPCC, Hugh Campbell, asked her if the social workers weren't correct to be concerned when the boy said he didn't want to go home because bad things happened to him there, and had then used a toy in an explicitly sexual way to illustrate his fear? Before he was taken from home, she said, he wouldn't have known what sex was, and she couldn't bear to think what had been drummed into him while he was away. She commented that children would say anything under pressure.

Her son had been an innocent, happy little boy, who drew frogmen under water, tanks and guns, not sexual figures, she said. Since his return home, she told the inquiry, he told her he had cried every night he was away because she wasn't there, and asked her over and over again why she hadn't written to him. She said he had nightmares for weeks, and it was months before he was able to talk to her about what had happened.

Mrs B also described claims by her son's foster mother that he had behaved in a very strange way, chanting about God, during a power cut, as 'a load of twaddle', and said she knew nothing about comments that her eleven-year-old daughter had behaved in an overtly sexual way on the plane that brought the children back home to Orkney.

The foster mother who had looked after Mrs B's two daughters during their time in care said both girls became distressed after a disclosure session at the RSSPCC Centre in Strathaven. She said the children were pressurised into admitting they had been sexually assaulted, and that the interviewers had told the girls they knew someone had hurt them. They'd also drawn a picture and said it was the younger girl, and asked her to point to the parts that Morris McKenzie had touched. The child told her foster mother she had pointed to her private parts because she thought that was what they wanted her to do. The elder girl was also shown a picture, but told the RSSPCC workers she didn't know who Morris McKenzie was and that he had never touched her. She asked them to leave her alone, said her foster mother, because they kept going on and on at her.

The boy's foster mother said he had wanted to stop going to the RSSPCC interview at Strathaven. 'He was fed up, he did not like going, he didn't want to go back, and he said they were wanting him to say things he didn't want to say,' she told the inquiry. She said the child had had to travel frequently to the house in Strathaven for the disclosure interviews, a journey lasting an hour, and once there he was often questioned for up to an hour and a half. She said all she could do was try to reassure him and tell him that going to the centre just had to be done. She told the RSSPCC QC Hugh Campbell that she found him a very strange child who told her bizarre stories she could not understand.

Mrs B described herself as a strict parent who believed in discipline, but denied that her own or any of the other children were frightened of her, which had been suggested to her during cross-questioning. Her three children, she said, still lived in fear of the social workers taking them away again.

She also described the attitudes of Paul Lee, Sue Millar and Gordon Sloan. She said Mr Lee was 'arrogant, cold, determined and lacking any emotion'. Mr Sloan's behaviour was, according to Mrs B, 'explosive, disturbed – a tyrant of a little man. It was almost as though he had something to hide. He was trying to keep us from speaking,' and she recalled an incident with the team leader, Sue Millar, who had told her that any toys she tried to send to her children would be used in evidence against her. 'I said they were just cuddlies for bedtime,' said Mrs B, 'but she repeated what she'd said and sniggered'.

Describing her family's ordeal on the morning of the children's removal, Mrs H told of her anger and her fear that her husband might suffer a fit. He had been diagnosed as having a brain tumour only a short time before, and she was frightened that the situation would make him worse. Mr H was not called as a witness. Mrs H told the inquiry she didn't know two of the other four families at all, and only knew one family by sight.

She also said she couldn't bear to communicate with someone who had 'legally kidnapped her children', and left all contact between her family and the Director of Social Work, Paul Lee, to be conducted by her solicitor. She said her children had been badly affected by their time in care, her son becoming more aggressive, and her daughter very insecure and unhappy. She praised the role of the press and media: 'They did a good job. I do not think we would have got the children back without their effort,' she said. She questioned the way in which her children were interviewed during their time in care, after being told that her eight-year-old daughter had made some disclosures which had caused concern, about 'bad people hurting children'. Asked if she would be worried about such information she said: 'If it came out of their mouths unprompted and of their own accord, yes,' and she said that some of the information that had come from the foster parents about her children was totally out of character for them.

Her son's foster mother later described his behaviour as 'disturbed' and said he did some things which 'turned her stomach'. On one occasion, she said, he had pretended to be in a coffin with blood smeared on his hands and feet, and she said he made constant references to a minister. During this evidence the boy's mother broke down and left the hall.

Another father said he had been lied to by the authorities about his children while they were in care. Mr T said he had been given 'stereotyped phrases' by a social worker that were 'inexact and untruthful'. His children had both been very emotionally upset by the whole experience, and his eight-year-old daughter had been stuffed with junk food and was not in the best of health, with her long hair uncared for and a mouth full of ulcers. His children felt they'd been abandoned, he said. Describing the morning of the uplift, he said the hostility around them was almost tangible, and he had been too shocked to take anything in. He recalled one man saying that his children were in moral danger, and he told the children himself that they were being taken away because of the help they had given to the W family.

Mrs T also gave a description of the early morning raid. She said she had been shocked, but not surprised, and had asked if this had something to do with the W family. She had been specifically named in the allegations by the three W children as having had sexual intercourse with children, and was asked by QC Hugh Campbell for the RSSPCC if there wasn't a reason for social workers to be suspicious over letters and cards she had sent to those children, especially one saying 'I love you'? She said there was no reason to be suspicious, even if it was a soppy thing to say. 'I am more concerned that they reduced love to a four letter word' she said, and added that it was entirely unreasonable of the Social Work Department to have concerns over her relationship with the W children.

None of the parents was in the witness box for more than a day and half, some for considerably less. Some believed the balance was weighed heavily against them, others stuck to their conviction that the due process of law would put everything right, and that if they had been able to go straight into court, without the Children's Hearing System, the situation would not have developed in the way it did.

Both the doctors involved in the medical examinations of the children after their removal from Orkney told Lord Clyde they had found no signs of sexual abuse in any of the nine children. The five children who were in care in Highland Region were examined two days after they had arrived, and all had given their verbal permission for the examinations. The other four, who were taken straight to the Royal Hospital for Sick Children at Yorkhill in Glasgow, were examined immediately on their arrival. Three out of the four had given permission, said the doctor, and the fourth had finally agreed, after further explanation.

When the inquiry resumed after the Christmas break, Lord Clyde heard that the children at the centre of the alleged child abuse investigation became more sexually aware because of questioning by care workers. A senior social worker from Strathclyde, Phil Greene, said that even if the children had not been abused, they would have been 'sexualised' by the system of investigation. He said that some of the foster-parents had told him their concerns over what the children felt was the 'grilling' they were subjected to at the disclosure sessions. One girl had said 'I was asked so often I got fed up with being asked, so I just said yes'.

Mr Greene described his unhappiness about some of his staff coming under the direction of Orkney Islands Council. His unease had grown after meeting Orkney's team leader, Sue Millar. He sympathised with the worries of his own social workers who were on the verge of pulling out on the eve of the uplift, and said he would have done the same thing in their shoes. 'I would want to ensure that what I was doing was legal, competent and safe before I took action,' he said. He added that the law put social workers in an impossible no-win situation in cases like this because there was a legal obligation on them to act even when they didn't have enough evidence to make the case stick in court.

The Chairman of the Social Work Committee, Councillor Mairhi Trickett told Lord Clyde that she didn't believe the inquiry would answer the questions that most people wanted answered. There would, she said, be enormous difficulties in returning to any sort of normality and restoring confidence in the community in South Ronaldsay. She described how she was informed of the allegations concerning the four families, and how she and Paul Lee had held a meeting to answer questions from her fellow councillors. They had, she said, been very antagonistic towards Mr Lee. She told, too, of the unpleasant letters and phone calls she herself had received, after the removal of the children, many of the letters anonymous, and many telephone calls between midnight and half past one in the morning.

Mrs Trickett was particularly critical of the media coverage. This had completely overwhelmed the social work staff, she said, who had described the media coverage as biased and unhelpful. She said she had some sympathy for the reporters, because they were only being given one side of the story, as the Social Work Department was bound by confidentiality. She had, she said, tried to give the reporters what information she could, in an attempt to redress the balance, but sometimes they did not want to hear the other side of the story and it was not reported.

In his evidence to the inquiry, the interim Reporter to Orkney Children's Panel criticised Sheriff Kelbie. Gordon Sloan said the Sheriff, in abandoning the case, had branded the three W children as liars, and had therefore dealt the case a death blow. 'If he had limited his comments to the competency point,' he said, 'we might have been able to reconstruct the case'. He seriously regretted having to take the decision to abandon his case against the parents, citing the publicity as one cause. But he maintained that the press coverage had not changed his own actions in any way at all.

Charged with domineering and tyrannical behaviour towards the parents by one of their advocates, John Doohan, Gordon Sloan said they were entitled to express their views. Donald Mackay, QC for Orkney Islands Council explained that such an answer was of no help to the inquiry and Lord Clyde pointed out that the wrong conclusion might be drawn. Mr Sloan denied that he had behaved in the way suggested. He described how one mother had stopped him at the top of the stairs in the Children's Panel offices and said she was going to stand and stare at him. He'd been expecting that kind of behaviour, he said, and felt embarrassed for her. 'I have conducted Hearings for twenty years and the ones here were no different to others,' he told the inquiry.

Mr Sloan told Lord Clyde he had chosen the word 'ritual' in connection with the alleged child abuse, very carefully, but he said that no suggestion of witchcraft or satanism was intended by the use of it. He wanted the inquiry to note that 'ritual' referred to the music and dancing that was supposed to have taken place during the outdoor sex sessions that three children already in care claimed took place on the island. 'I looked for an alternative word but there didn't seem to be one,' he said, 'it did not refer to any abuse'.

Mr Sloan also told the inquiry of the other factors that led to his decision to abandon the hearing of proof. Sheriff Kelbie's remarks as he had dismissed the case, he said, were issued 'like a press release', but there were other reasons for his decision. By the time a new case could have come to court, said the Reporter, the children would have been at home for some time, and they would be subject to pressure from their parents to keep silent about any abuse they might have suffered. In addition, the mother of the W children was being allowed to visit them in their foster homes on the mainland, and he felt the children who had made the allegations that led to the removal of nine others, might be persuaded to 'close down', that is not to talk, so the prospect of them providing the court with any information, he said, was non-existent.

Gordon Sloan also criticised the lawyers acting for the parents who had placed confidential medical information before the Children's Panel. He said this was inappropriate, and added that the medicals would not, in any case, have been able to show up what he had alleged in the grounds of referral. These, he told the inquiry, referred only to the children being in 'moral danger' and to 'simulated sexual acts'. He also said that he had feared that the alleged abuse would recur if the children were returned to their homes. The grounds of referral, he said, suggested that these were children whose parents, as well as other members of the community, were involved in abuse, and that, in his view, was sufficient for the children to be kept in some form of detention.

Calling for the press and media to be banned from Children's Hearings, Mr Sloan said they had acted irresponsibly in this case. They had, he said, consistently misreported events on Orkney while the nine children were in care.

The Reporter was asked if he had failed to exercise his legal duties to protect the nine children after Sheriff Kelbie had dismissed the case. If there were grounds for believing abuse had occurred before it began, nothing had changed. Mr Sloan said that in his view it was in the best interests of the children for them to remain in care, but after the Sheriff's judgment, he felt he had no option but to allow them to return home.

The Orkney children themselves were not given any reasons by social workers why they were being taken into care. Dr John Powell, the consultant psychiatrist appointed to give evidence on their behalf, told the inquiry the children had no idea why they were taken away from their homes. Some had been told they would be away for a day, others that it would be seven days, and all of them had told him they would never trust social workers in their lives again. One girl told him she grew to hate them, as they never listened to what she said.

Dr Powell, from the Crichton Royal Hospital in Dumfries, talked to the children in December 1991, at around the time their parents were giving evidence at the inquiry. One eight-year-old girl, who had been described by social workers as 'unnaturally controlled' told him: 'I was beyond tears. I couldn't cry. I was too unhappy.' Another little girl, whose behaviour had regressed considerably after being away for five weeks, had nightmares about monsters surrounding her almost nightly on her return. She told Dr Powell she would never seek help from the authorities, and described them as 'horrible'. On her return to South Ronaldsay this little girl told her best friend: 'social workers locked me in a cage and wouldn't let me see my parents', Dr Powell told the inquiry. He said this child was especially anxious that she might be taken away again.

The two older girls had said they would like to give evidence at the inquiry themselves. They would like to 'say their piece' they told him. They all said the social workers did not believe them when they denied that sexual abuse had taken place, and the oldest of the nine children, a fifteen-year-old boy, said he was subject to mental abuse by the social workers who interviewed him. Dr Powell described this boy as 'an angry young man who feels that those responsible for what happened should be punished'.

An eight-year-old boy said he hadn't known why he was taken away from home, and added: 'I don't even know now.' His eleven-year-old sister remembered being taken away as a 'tug-of-war' between her mother and a social worker, with herself in the middle. She said she was sometimes deliberately unco-operative during the interview sessions and threw soft toys at the workers. Her older sister said she believed the inquiry would find that the authorities had 'done a very wrong thing'.

The fifteen-year-old said he remembered being told by his interviewers that they did not believe his denials, and this made him angry. He told Dr Powell that he had been worried that he and his brother might be taken away by social workers because of his parents' support for the W family. His younger brother told the doctor that he felt the social workers didn't trust him, and he also hoped that those involved would suffer some form of punishment or humiliation. He said that the interviewers had tried to get information out of him by saying: 'If you give us just one name we'll tell you how a helicopter works. We will go and get fish and chips if you tell us.' He had been told to draw a circle with a man in the middle and was asked if he ever did any dancing.

A twelve-year-old boy told Dr Powell: 'It was not true what they said about us.' He was referring, the psychiatrist told the inquiry, to the interviews carried out by police officers and officials from the RSSPCC. The boy said: 'They tried to convince me something happened, that we did dance in the quarry and things. They drew a ring of people with somebody in the middle. They asked me, did I know who was in the middle? Did I like the minister? Was there somebody with a cloak and did I know who it was?'; and he told Dr Powell that the interviewers had said bad things about his parents. He said he'd lost his temper with the interviewers and thrown things at them, and he was worried about being taken into care again.

Dr Powell told the inquiry many common features had emerged from his interviews with the children; the separation from their families was completely unexpected and traumatic in varying degrees; they didn't know where they were going, who they were to stay with, or how long they'd be away; they all felt hostile towards social workers, who had appeared very biased against their parents, and they wouldn't trust the profession in the future; the interviewers did not believe them when they denied any knowledge of sex abuse, nor did they listen to what they had to say; they'd all suffered regressive behaviour and sleep disturbance when they returned home, and they were angered and embarrassed by the medical examinations.

Most of the children, Dr Powell said, had few complaints about their foster homes or foster parents, but some had considered running away. They'd decided against this, as they didn't know how they'd get home. They had also told him that any drawings produced during the disclosure sessions were not done by the children spontaneously, but were suggested by the interviewers.

One of those interviewers, RSSPCC social worker Liz McLean, was in the witness box for thirteen days. She had conducted the disclosure therapy sessions with the W children, and it was from the statements of three of them that the allegations had come. These three were aged seven, eight and nine. She described them as 'so high they were bouncing off the walls' when they were taken to the RSSPCC centre for interview. They'd been suspicious too, she said, checking out the centre for hidden alarms and cameras, and it had been impossible to tape-record the interviews for that reason.

Mrs McLean told the inquiry that the children drew pictures on rolls of wallpaper to illustrate the stories they were telling, and they told her and WPC Linda Williamson that children were sexually abused in a quarry by the local minister, the Reverend Morris McKenzie. They said the minister had then encouraged other adults to have sex with children, and that music was playing from a hi-fi.

The eight-year-old at one point during the interview turned to Liz McLean and asked: 'Do you know this was all a lie?' but Mrs McLean told the inquiry she believed the child was just 'testing' her to see if she understood what she was saying. The child had smiled, and Liz McLean said she had smiled back as encouragingly as she could. She told the inquiry that the child had said one thing, but meant another. This was on 20 February, and it was only seven days later that the nine South Ronaldsay children were taken from their homes at 7 o'clock in the morning.

From the interviews came stories of turtle costumes, cowboy suits and a man in a black cloak 'hooking' children into the centre of a ring. Mrs McLean told the inquiry, too, of enormous amounts of mail sent to the W children, containing what she called 'trigger words'; words like Brownies, rainbows, love-hearts and turtles. These had all seemed to be out of context. She told the inquiry that the three children had had no contact with each other for several weeks, and that their disclosures contained so many similar statements that she was convinced they were telling the truth. She denied coaching them.

She was cross-examined about the interviewing techniques she used, but denied that she had been probing the children in an attempt to establish that there was a paedophile ring in South Ronaldsay, nor, she said, had she looked for coded messages in the sackfuls of mail which arrived from Orkney. Suggesting she had asked leading questions, QC Edward Targowski quoted some of the points she had put to the children, taken from the transcripts and naming a number of adults and other children. She admitted that her wording at times was not particularly good.

Liz McLean told the inquiry that she was responsible for interviewing five of the nine children removed from their homes on 27 February. These were the five who were fostered in Highland Region, and she stressed she had nothing to do with the other four, who were in Strathclyde. She did, however, relay details of what those four had been saying in interviews, to Orkney's Social Work Department although she had never looked through the transcripts of those interviews. QC Edward Targowski said this meant the way the information travelled from Strathclyde to Orkney – via Mrs McLean – was totally artificial.

Evidence emerged of how some of the nine children had made statements to Mrs McLean or to police officers that appeared to support the allegations of the three W children. Some of the details about dancing in a circle, with a 'master' or 'prime minister' in the centre seemed to back up the original stories. Mrs McLean was asked if it was intended that the interviews should introduce any of the details disclosed by the W children, that is to lead the children along the lines of the previous disclosures. She said it was not. She said the information was given voluntarily and that the children were not coached by anyone.

She claimed that an eight-year-old girl had drawn a circle of people with the man in the middle wearing a cloak, and that he pulled children into the middle with a hook. The child had said she felt very sad and hurt and asked for it to stop. Mrs McLean said the child wanted the man prosecuted and sent to jail, and when she asked her why the children hadn't told people about the abuse the child said: 'We don't know all the words to say what happened.'

'That struck me as a very mature and thoughtful thing for her to have said,' said Liz McLean.

It emerged that Liz McLean had carried out a total of forty interviews with the five South Ronaldsay children in thirteen days. She denied this was an excessive amount, or that the children had been put under too much pressure. The frequency of interviews, she told Donald MacFadyen, QC to the inquiry, was very much determined by the child, and that interviews could take place every second day if the child wished. The inquiry heard that a nine-year-old boy was interviewed ten times in all, while his eight-year-old sister and another girl the same age were seen eight times. Taking the boy as an example, she said he was actually questioned for only about half the time he was with them, the rest of the time he played. She said he was ready to start talking about sex abuse when the Reporter, Gordon Sloan, brought the sessions to an end.

Regarding a twelve-year-boy who resolutely denied any abuse ever having taken place, Liz McLean rejected a suggestion that he was forced to come to the interview sessions against his will. QC Edward Targowski asked if the children really had any choice in the matter at all. He said the twelve-year-old had been noted as being 'very scared' and had told the interviewers he did not like coming to see them, but despite that he was told they still wanted to see him on a weekly basis. 'How can that be giving a child free choice?' he asked. 'That was checked out with the child,' replied Mrs McLean. 'There are times when the child can say no and when he will look at you and indicate that he wants to come.' Mr Targowski also wondered how Mrs McLean could keep an open mind when interviewing the South Ronaldsay children when she believed they had been abused.

Replying to criticism of her interviewing methods by Dr Judith Trowel, a consultant psychiatrist from London, Liz McLean urged the inquiry to listen to the tapes of her interviews with the children. This, she said, would enable them to put the questioning into its proper context better than the transcripts. The psychiatrist, who was later called as an independent witness, noted that one interview in particular, with an eight-year-old girl, was full of confused material. Mrs McLean said she didn't accept the criticism. Mr Targowski told the inquiry that when the child said: 'Nothing ever happened to me,' it was quite clear. Liz McLean said: 'That could be because she has given just a bit too much and she is moving back a bit. I think she spontaneously described quite a number of things that would say she knew a lot,' and she insisted that the five children she was reponsible for interviewing all wanted to come back for more sessions with her.

The inquiry heard that police notes of at least one interview confused things said by two different children; Liz McLean said she had relied on the police notes for her information, and had passed that on to team leader Sue Millar in Orkney. She also described her 'shock' when the interview sessions were brought to an abrupt and premature halt. 'The children were communicating and had a need to communicate more about certain things,' she said. They had built up a good relationship with the social workers and police officers and she had wanted to continue her work with them. She told Hugh Campbell, QC for her employers, the RSSPCC, that abused children who are returned home often get back in touch with the agency who has interviewed them.

WPC Linda Williamson, who had assisted Liz McLean during the interviewing sessions, followed her into the witness box. She, too, described the disclosures of the W children which pointed to a sex ring in South Ronaldsay involving the Reverend Morris McKenzie and other adults. She told the inquiry she had attended two police courses on child abuse, and had been involved in a number of police inquiries into the matter, but she called for more police training in this field, and said she knew of no woman police officer in the Northern Constabulary who would have had the experience to carry out interviews, as laid down in the 'Effective Intervention' document from the Scottish Officer, or in the Cleveland Report.

She disagreed with her RSSPCC colleague over the implications of the mail sent to the W children in care, and believed a lot of it was very innocent. 'To me a Brownie uniform is a Brownie uniform and a teddy bear is a teddy bear,' she said. The inquiry had already heard that hundreds of letters and Christmas presents had been kept from the W children they were intended for. WPC Williamson also said that Liz McLean had 'pushed' the children more than she herself would have done, and she agreed that Mrs McLean had asked a leading question of one of the W children, but asked by QC Donald Mackay how she could have allowed it, she replied: 'I don't know.'

Referring to the nine children taken from Orkney at the end of February, she expressed her 'grave doubts' about whether one boy in particular had been involved in the alleged 'sex romps' at all. His continual denials had caused her serious misgivings, and she said he believed he was being persecuted because of his family's support for the W family. He was very distressed and anxious to go home all the time, she told the inquiry. She admitted to QC Edward Targowski that some of her note-taking had been careless, but that she was still convinced that the stories from the W children had been true.

Other evidence given by RSSPCC workers and police showed that some of the nine children believed they had been taken from their homes because of a grudge against the English. There had been anger from the children, but directed at the people who had taken them away, not at their parents. The fifteen-year-old believed he had fewer rights than if he had been in jail, and the twelve-year-old girl described all the claims as 'utter rubbish'. One RSSPCC worker, Lindsay Stevenson, said she had made secret tapes of the interviews with some of the nine children, and admitted to the inquiry that this was an act of dishonesty which could have affected the relationship of trust she was trying to build up with the children. Commenting on the criticism of interviewing techniques by the London psychiatrist, Dr Judith Trowel, who said the interviews began with information and leading questions, Miss Stevenson said she had introduced ideas they wanted to explore, by way of explaining why the children had been taken into care. She completely refuted the statement in Dr Trowel's report which said: 'This is a superb example of how not to do an investigative interview'.

In February 1992 the Church of Scotland minister at the centre of many of the allegations of child abuse in South Ronaldsay, was told that the inquiry did not want to hear his side of the story, and that it was not necessary for him to testify. The Scottish Office, in a letter to the Reverend Morris McKenzie, said that any evidence he would be able to give would fall outside the remit of Lord Clyde's inquiry. Similar letters were sent to members of the Parents' Action Group, and it was left to them to make either oral or written submissions to the inquiry, which would not be treated as evidence.

These included the chairman, Dr Helen Martini, the children's GP, Dr Richard Broadhurst, and South Ronaldsay Councillor Cyril Annal. He commented that no one from the island had been asked to speak at the inquiry, and he thought it was important that at least one local person was called. At this point Isles MP Jim Wallace intervened, and the inquiry decided to invite these three members of the island community to give evidence.

Revd McKenzie's advocate, Graham Robertson, told Lord Clyde that the minister was anxious to redress the balance of evidence against him. His name had been mentioned almost every day since December, often in the most sinister light, said Mr Robertson, but he felt the terms of the inquiry would not allow him to challenge the statements made about him. Mrs McKenzie was fiercely critical and gave an interview to journalists she believed to be 'responsible and professional' persons. She said her husband should be allowed the chance to clear his name. She had felt that as she was not a party to the inquiry, or a witness, she was free to give the interview. Mr McKenzie himself, said Mr Robertson, did not know of her intention to speak to the press until afterwards.

Dr Helen Martini, Chairman of the South Ronaldsay Parents' Action Group, called at the last moment to give evidence, told the inquiry of the absolute panic on South Ronaldsay and the feeling that human rights had been infringed. She described how anger had grown at the way the nine children had been treated, and how she and others had been determined that the four sets of parents should not be branded as 'social outcasts'. She said they were not judging the innocence or guilt of the parents, but were concerned for the children's welfare.

'Whether the parents were innocent or guilty was for the law to decide,' she said, 'I presumed most of us in the community felt that they were innocent, but we felt that the main injustice was the way the children had been treated.' She told the inquiry it was obvious from the start that there had been no multi-agency, multi-disciplinary approach to the operation.

Councillor Cyril Annal, who represented the South Ronaldsay community, said he felt at the outset that the Social Work Department had made a monumental blunder. He said he was continually 'fobbed off' by the Social Work Director, Paul Lee, when he tried to find out exactly why the nine children had been taken into care. He also told the inquiry that, three weeks before the uplift, he had been tipped off by a fellow councillor that something was going to happen. Social Work Chairman, Councillor Mairhi Trickett had, he said, 'seemed quite excited' and had told him to stay away from the father of two of the children who were later taken away, but he told the inquiry he had not been officially informed that the dawn raids were to take place, even on the morning the children were removed.

Councillor Annal called for Paul Lee to be removed from his post as director, saying that as long as he remained, the people of South Ronaldsay would never have any confidence in the Social Work Department, and he told Lord Clyde: 'You have no idea how the community were terrorised. I have never seen people so frightened.'

Isles MP Jim Wallace and Scottish Office ministers were told in advance of the plans to remove the children, but a former social work adviser to the Secretary of State said they should never be taken away from their homes without enough evidence to stand up in court. It was also admitted by a senior Scottish Office official that the case had highlighted shortcomings in the government guidelines on child-care.

Dr Judith Trowel from the Tavistock clinic in London, as well as criticising the interviewing techniques used by the RSSPCC workers, also criticised their choice as interviewers at all. They had been involved in talking to the W children, so could not have been open-minded, she claimed. She said it was bad practice for interviewers to have drawn pictures for the children and told them what other children had said. She also told the inquiry that a way should have been found for the Orkney children to have been told that their parents were alive and well. It would have been in their best interests, she said, for them to have some contact.

Orkney's Social Work Director Paul Lee, who was the inquiry's first witness, was also its last. He was called to clear up some points that had arisen during the course of the investigation, and to answer a query about his memory of events. It was suggested to him that, in view of the crisis in his department, and the all-round stress, that his recollection might be faulty, but he replied that his memory was no less reliable than anyone else's, and he called for an outside person to be appointed to act as an intermediary between Social Work Departments and parents in such cases. He called, too, for bridges to be built in Orkney and for the 'healing process' to begin.

The inquiry then adjourned until 5 May when four oral submissions would be heard, including one from Mrs Jan McKenzie, wife of the minister who had been so villified during the giving of evidence. Written submissions would follow. The other three were

Mrs Kathleen Marshall, Director of the Scottish Child Law Centre, Mr Gerard Brown of the Glasgow Bar Association, and Mrs Donella Kirkland, an Orkney resident.

Mrs Marshall called for a radical change in Scots Law in the wake of the Orkney case. She called for a Children's Act for Scotland which would put the interests of the child first, and said this legislation should be based on the United Nations Convention on the rights of the child.

Mrs McKenzie accused social workers of twisting everyday happenings and linking them to satanic or sexual abuse, and said the symbols of her husband's ministry had been interpreted as satanic by social workers bent on proving a theory. They had failed, she said, to make reasonably adequate inquiries into the possible innocent explanations of the allegations made against the four families and other people involved in the South Ronaldsay case. She claimed that many of the events that had sparked off the uplift of the children had been social functions in the community, such as Hallowe'en parties and other events organised by the church, the Parent Teacher Association, and other youth organisations. These, she said, often involved dressing up in fancy dress costumes. She criticised the sinister connotations put on the cards and letters sent to children in care, and said these were a normal part of everyday living.

Gerard Brown, of the Glasgow Bar Association, questioned the ability of Children's Hearings to deal with the complexities of child abuse, and claimed that the fact that they were composed of lay people was often a weakness. He called for such cases to be removed from the Hearing System.

The Orkney resident, Mrs Donella Kirkland, the last person to address the inquiry, said she was absolutely stunned at the manner in which the Social Work Department and the police had behaved, and she had, she said, warned her own children that they could be taken away and questioned by social workers. 'In view of what happened, I felt that nobody, whether or not they were innocent or guilty, was able to look at their own front door and feel it was adequate protection,' she said. Mrs Kirkland praised the role of the media and rejected the suggestion that they had whipped up a sensational story out of nothing. She said that as the mother of four children, she knew that children were very prone to confuse fact and fiction. The philosophy of most social workers working in the field, though, seemed to be 'believe the child'. That she maintained, had led to the chaos they had seen in Orkney. She urgently appealed for the people of Orkney to get together and heal the wounds in the community, and she called for a public apology from social workers as a first step to reconciliation.

When she had finished her oral submission, Lord Clyde told her: 'It is a sign of hope that you have aired the kind of views you have. It is for the community to get together.'

As the inquiry ended with a further fifty-five written submissions, and the closing submissions by the lawyers, Lord Clyde was urged not to produce a 'whitewash report', and a 'revolution' in child sex abuse training was called for.

After 135 days, making it the second longest public inquiry in Scottish legal history, the inquiry ended. It had cost the tax-payer around £6 million and sixty-nine witnesses had testified. At the end of it all, the public perception of its worth seemed questionable, with the commonest phrase heard amongst islanders being 'waste of time', and a realisation that the truth would probably never be known.

The waiting time for Lord Clyde's report began.

CHAPTER SIXTEEN

Lord Clyde Reports

On 27 October 1992 Lord Clyde's 'Report of the Inquiry into the Removal of Children from Orkney in February 1991' was published. In the middle of the afternoon, the Secretary of State for Scotland, Ian Lang, made a statement to the House of Commons, and then the 363-page report became a public document. There had been no leaked information from the report, although well-informed speculation in some of the national papers had set the scene for the many recommendations the report contained. Some of the families feared it would be a 'whitewash', others believed the processes of law would prevail, and one mother said that throughout the eight-month-long inquiry Lord Clyde 'hadn't missed a trick'. She had watched him carefully throughout, she said, and had pinned all her trust on his findings.

Her trust was not misplaced. It appeared that Lord Clyde had missed nothing. The Remit of the Inquiry was never to investigate the truth or otherwise of the allegations, so none of the parents could expect their names to be cleared by the Report. Lord Clyde said, however, that the Scottish principle of presumption of innocence should apply, and he went on to criticise nearly everyone involved in the removal of the children in February 1991: 'It is not easy to find any individual, at least among the principal actors out of the whole story of events relating to the removal of the nine children, who is not open to some criticism . . . The purpose of this Inquiry has not been to find guilt or innocence or to distribute praise or blame but rather in recognising that things may have gone wrong, to endeavour to learn from past mistakes and to make suggestions as to how such mistakes may not be repeated in the future.'

The criticisms of nearly everyone involved in the planning and management of the case were stringent. Starting with the W family, Lord Clyde said the Social Work Department failed to keep a wholly open mind regarding the allegations made by three of the children, and allowed their thinking to be coloured by undefined suspicions which they failed to explore. The department had failed to resolve the growing antagonism between themselves and the friends of Mrs W, and saw it solely as hostility towards the Social Work Department.

The lack of guidelines and procedures on child sexual abuse was also criticised – the Department failed to follow the guidance of the Scottish Office document, Effective Intervention, or the Cleveland Report.

LORD CLYDE REPORTS

183

Because of this they failed to hold a multi-disciplinary conference at any early stage to assess and analyse the evidence, and to determine the proper course of action.

There was repeated reference throughout the Report to the lack of proper records of meetings, communications, discussions, planning decisions and other matters related to the removal and interviewing of the nine children. Lord Clyde was especially critical that the Social Work Department failed to make any adequate record of the decision to remove the children, that detailed information wasn't available for the social workers coming in from Strathclyde, that information on and about the children themselves was scant, that there were many inaccuracies in the Acting Reporter's paper-work, and that he kept no written record of his own work, and that those involved in interviewing the children while they were in care, also failed to keep proper records of the interviews. Inadequate, inappropriate and failure are the three words which appear most often in the Report. Lord Clyde said the evaluation of the allegations made by the W children was inadequate, and no thought was given as to whether the removal of the nine children was appropriate. He said Orkney's Social Work Department moved immediately from hearing the allegations to the decision to take out Place of Safety Orders. Logically, it did not follow that because the allegations had to be taken seriously they had to be believed, and there was a failure on the part of members of the staffs of the Social Work Department, the RSSPCC and the police to distinguish adequately between the two.

Lord Clyde said that more care had to be taken where the only allegation of abuse comes from a third party and even more enquiries were required to determine whether those nine children were in any danger. The children the Social Work Department and the police were proposing to remove were children who, said the Report, had made no complaint themselves of any abuse, and it was only on the word of other children that the authorities were proceeding. The Social Work Department failed to give sufficient weight to the fact that the allegations did not come directly from the nine allegedly abused children. In addition, the department and the RSSPCC failed to carry out any detailed analysis of the information they received. The management of the Social Work Department were well aware of the history of the W family, and that the children who had made the allegations had come from a family with a history of abuse which was likely to have affected their development. Lord Clyde said that what might have seemed real to them might well not accord with what was real to others.

Not only were the allegations inadequately assessed, said the Report, but those managing the case failed properly to assess the risk to which the nine children might be exposed. The grounds for supposing that any repetition of the alleged abuse was about to occur were speculative, and Lord Clyde said that certainly it could not be seriously contemplated that any immediate action was necessary for the safety of the children. There was a complete failure to analyse the need for Place of Safety Orders on an individual basis for each child. At every stage of planning, and in the presentation before the Sheriff, the Social Work Department had failed to treat each child as an individual. He criticised the Team Leader Mrs Sue Millar for failing to set out the position as it applied to each child before the Sheriff.

No other courses of action other than removal were considered, said the Report. At no stage did anyone stop to question or review the course on which they were engaged: 'The Social Work Department acted too hastily in determining to remove the children and failed to take time to pause and think before embarking on precipitate action.' He criticised the failure to appoint a case manager, and said that with no adequate inter-agency discussion the major decision – to remove the children – was taken as a matter of almost instant reaction as if those taking it were acting under a sense of panic rather than with a measured consideration. He said the criticism of this course of action should be shared between the Social Work Department and the Northern Constabulary, who endorsed the decision.

Lord Clyde criticised the Social Work Director, Paul Lee, for failing to consider the cost, the administrative complexities and the later care of the children before taking action. He pointed out, too, the need to reassess the whole evidence after the results of the medical examinations became known. These results ought to have raised a very serious doubt in the minds both of the Reporter and the Social Work Department. But no reappraisal was made, and the Acting Reporter, Gordon Sloan, successfully opposed any attention being paid to the medical examinations before the hearings. That was another matter for Lord Clyde to criticise: 'If they had stopped to consider the situation and investigated further it is improbable that they would at that stage have removed the nine children.'

Mrs Sue Millar was further criticised for inadequate communication with the social workers from Strathclyde who were to assist in the removal operation. These professionals went to Orkney expecting to be far more deeply involved in the case than transpired. Lord Clyde said that Mrs Millar's indication to them that the adults would be arrested gave the Strathclyde workers a false impression of the strength of the police view of the case. She also indicated that further information would be made available to them, but in the event this was not forthcoming. The Report refers to the growing unease of the mainland workers about the sufficiency of grounds for the whole operation. Again, no formal records were kept regarding the meetings with the incoming workers, and Lord Clyde said Mrs Millar was faced with a formidable task which it was beyond her capacity to carry out. He referred to her poor relationships within the Social Work Department, and her naturally somewhat abrupt manner, which discouraged questioning from staff.

Lord Clyde was critical of the fact that there was so little information available about the children, their state of development, medical background and other facts which the foster carers should have had access to. He also criticised the total lack of information given to the children about their placements so that they knew what to expect. The Social Work Department, he said, did not adequately plan the arrangements for the children after the stage of removal, and they failed completely to provide any support for the parents after the children were taken away. Despite the likelihood of opposition and even hostility, said the Report, planning should have taken place for an early and direct contact with the parents of the nine children.

The Social Work Department failed to refer the matter to the Acting Reporter until the children were removed on 27 February. Although Mr Sloan was aware of the situation some days previously, he chose to follow the procedure adopted in Strathclyde under which no action was required of him until the referral was made. The Report said the Social Work Department might well have thought of seeking his advice at the earliest stage and the idea that a Reporter cannot act until a case is 'referred' to him was not based on the statute, but on practice. Mr Sloan should have taken action earlier, then the Children's Hearing could have been held on the first lawful day after the removal, which is required by statute. It was highly prejudicial to the parents and the children to deny them the immediate opportunity to have the removal considered by a Children's Hearing. Lord Clyde also said that the Acting Reporter should have exercised greater patience and control in his conduct of matters at the hearings.

The Report did not criticise either the timing or the manner of the removal. The workers involved were described as efficient and supportive, showing a high level of professional skill and consideration, but Lord Clyde said the children should have been allowed to discuss what was happening and why, and that their rights should have been respected. The children themselves, he said, had been concerned at the short time they had to say goodbye to their parents, and that they were not allowed to take any personal possessions with them. He criticised the lack of time the parents had to study the Place of Safety Orders before they were removed, and said it would have been easy to make copies so that each of the four families could have kept a copy to study after the removal. Also, the parents should have been asked to sign written consent forms for the medical examinations, and there was no sound reason why information about the medical condition of the children should not have been passed to the parents.

Lord Clyde also criticised some of the placements selected for the children; Geilsland School was totally inappropriate for the 15 year old boy, even as a temporary refuge, and urban locations for the B children in Strathclyde, so very different from the island of South Ronaldsay, could only be unsettling. The selection of the Highland Region placements, he said, were chosen with care.

There were, however, inadequate grounds for separating siblings from each other. Lord Clyde said the reason for the separations was substantially related to the securing of evidence from them, and that the welfare of the children was subordinated to the interest of obtaining evidence. In addition the ban on all access simply added to the children's sense of isolation. The judge said access by letter or telephone by the parents and older members of the family should have been allowed, and he saw no reason why adult siblings could not visit their two younger brothers. The parents should also have been told the whereabouts of their children. Also the Social Work Department should not have interfered with correspondence addressed to the children, and the children should have been encouraged to write home, not discouraged as they were in some cases.

The Report stated that neither Orkney's Social Work Department, the police, nor the RSSPCC undertook detailed planning for the investigation of the allegations, and in particular for the part which interviewing of the nine children might play in that investigation. The planning should have covered the adequacy of the resources to carry out the interviewing, as well as a joint strategy for the conduct of the interviews. Above all attention should have been given to the possible need for a more detailed assessment of the children, in particular of their mental and developmental status. This, he said, was a failure which had already occurred in relation to the W children.

The number and timing of interviews was also unplanned, and no time allowed for the interviewers to prepare, discuss, reflect and record the results of the interviews. Lord Clyde said that Mrs Liz MacLean's willingness to take on most of the work set the tone for the RSSPCC's failure to recognise that the interviewing of the nine children might run a considerable risk of being conducted in a less than satisfactory manner. The Report also said that the dangers of employing interviewers who had already been involved with the W children should have been appreciated. The Social Work Department, the police and the RSSPCC all failed to consider fully the propriety of this, and Mrs Liz MacLean, Miss Lindsey Stevenson and Constable Linda Williamson were all involved with both sets of children.

Lord Clyde criticised the training standards attained by the RSSPCC interviewers and the lack of senior management control in RSSPCC practices. The police interviewers were also described as being inadequately trained. The methods and procedures for interviewing children lacked clarity, and the resulting reports were inadequate. The RSSPCC standard interviewing technique was described as inappropriate for investigative work. The interviewers also failed to deal with denials of the allegations by any of the children. There had been no planning on how to deal with denials, and Lord Clyde said this illustrated the extent to which the interviewers did not maintain an open mind. Moreover, he said, stress on their belief that the allegations were true, might easily have led the children to consider there was little point in saying anything that contradicted what the interviewers had said, as they might feel they would not be believed.

Lord Clyde also said that leading questions were asked during many of the interviews with the nine children, by both the RSSPCC and police interviewers, and said the use of leading questions to elicit information is recognised as evidentially hazardous. Some of the children were interviewed very intensively, without any planning of the duration or frequency, and Lord Clyde criticised the failure of the agencies to explain fully to the children what the purpose of the interviews was.

The return of the children to Orkney on 4 April was precipitate, but justifiable in the circumstances, according to the Report. But it also criticised the Acting Reporter for his decision to abandon the Proof proceedings. This decision, said Lord Clyde, was open to debate. The Court of Session had opened the way for the proof to be heard before another Sheriff after it upheld Gordon Sloan's Appeal against Sheriff Kelbie's decision. Lord Clyde did not agree that any evidence to support the case would have been tainted or irrecoverable, and it was not easy to reconcile the Acting Reporter's belief that the grounds for referral were well founded, with his abandonment of the case.

There were no findings on the effects of the affair on the children, nor on Revd Morris Mackenzie who had been at the centre of the allegations. The Inquiry had not been empowered to examine those things.

Lord Clyde said that although no one could be exempt from criticism he believed all those involved in the removal of the children had acted in good faith, and there was little advantage in criticism without constructive proposals: 'Underneath every system', he said, 'are the people implementing it. People are human. To err is one of the aspects of human life . . . I doubt if any system could be made so foolproof that no mistakes could be made. What I am seeking in the Report to suggest are steps that might at least reduce the risk of them ever being made.'

CHAPTER SEVENTEEN

Conclusions

Lord Clyde made 194 recommendations, designed to form the basis for a comprehensive and radical review of child care in Scotland. Calling for reform not recrimination, the recommendations mirrored the catalogue of criticism. The Report called for changes in the field of child law, and in particular child protection, with reference to both the European Convention on Human Rights and to the UN Convention on the Rights of the Child which was ratified with qualifications by the UK government on 16 December 1991.

Stating that there could be no doubt that power should exist under statute for the removal of a child to a place of safety, Lord Clyde stressed that the only occasion when this should happen was where there was a real, urgent and immediate risk that the child is going to suffer significant harm, whether physical, moral or psychological. He called for the provisions for Place of Safety Orders to be more tightly drawn, and said that in this he was sharing the view of the Association of Directors of Social Work.

For the purpose of the Report, referring to the Orders as Child Protection Orders, Lord Clyde said that the Sheriff or JP granting the Orders must have sight of the whole of the evidence and be satisfied that there is reasonable cause to believe that the child is likely to suffer significant harm if not removed. The critical consideration must be the imminence of risk, not the conclusion that any allegations of abuse or ill-treatment are established. Lord Clyde further said that where the case is of suspected sexual abuse, the Order should, if practicable, be obtained from a Sheriff, and that the area of the work dealing with Child Protection Orders should be the responsibility of the Sheriff. Also, that the parent or guardian and the child should have an immediate opportunity to have the Order varied or cancelled by the Sheriff. This would be at any time within seven days after the removal of the child, and such provision was necessary if the rights of children and their parents were to be fully recognised.

Lord Clyde further recommended that consideration should be given to the review and revisal of the work of the Children's Hearings in the area of child protection, with the possibility of two Panel Members sitting as assessors with the Sheriff in particularly complex cases. He also called for the appointment of an independent person with a wider role than that of a safeguarder, in order to protect the child's interests, and that all local

CONCLUSIONS 189

authorities should look for people able and willing to serve in that role, and arrange training for them.
Training was one of the vital elements in the Report. Lord Clyde called for an increase in the facilities for training in social work and in particular for specialist training over the whole area of child care. He recommended that the present two-year qualification course for social workers be increased to three, stressing this was an essential element in improving the service provided by the social work profession in this field. He said that local and central government should consider resourcing this training as a matter of priority.

The Report asked for a uniformity of approach to investigative interviewing, and said guidelines on the subject should be prepared centrally. It was recommended that the Social Work Services Group should prepare the guidelines, but that they should not be a substitute for good training and practice. Improved recording techniques and consistency of approach and practice were also called for.

Lord Clyde also said that more extensive police training should be provided, particularly in the work of interviewing children, and he called for joint training to be provided with ALL agencies involved in child care work.

Referring to the role of the media, Lord Clyde said that the Cleveland Report had called for the Press and the public to give social workers the support needed to continue in the work which the public requires of them. That message, he said, deserved to be repeated. He also recommended that consideration be given on whether to introduce further restraints on press reporting of proceedings before Children's Hearings and in the Sheriff Court in children's cases, but he said that the Press should be encouraged to increase public understanding of the problems of child sexual abuse and child protection work.

The Report was broadly welcomed on all sides of the House of Commons, with the Secretary of State saying it was justifiably critical of how things were handled, and that he was immediately accepting more than three-quarters of the recommendations. He said there was likely to be action on the rest after consultation.

He said training for child protection was of major importance and announced an immediate extra £40,000 for specialist training for social workers in the Scottish islands. But the very next day he caused outrage amongst all those campaigning for better training, including social workers and their representative organisations, by ruling it out on grounds of cost. The British Association of Social Workers said it was not now a question of whether the country could afford it, but whether they could afford not to do it, as the additional responsibilities having to be met could no longer be crushed into a two-year training programme.

So is the government only willing to support those recommendations with no cost implications? Some commented that the £6 million of public money spent on the Inquiry would have been better spent on improving training provision, and in the House of Commons, the MP for Perth and Kinross, Sir Nicholas Fairbairn, said that to have an Inquiry at that cost, that length, and with that number of lawyers involved, the one question it was about – the allegations of child sexual abuse – was not allowed to be discussed. This, he said, was absurd.

Orkney Islands Council reacted with shock to Lord Clyde's report. The Chairman of the Social Work Department, Mrs Mairhi Trickett, said: 'The degree of hostility and criticism my staff have had to endure has made their position extremely difficult. I do believe they have the most difficult job. They are damned if they don't do anything and damned if they do.' The council announced it would be conducting its own internal investigation, although that calls into question the point of the Inquiry. On Friday 30th October the Council Convener, Jackie Tait, after an all-day private meeting, said that the Council unequivocally accepted Lord Clyde's view that the parents and children involved, and the Reverend and Mrs McKenzie must be accorded the presumption of innocence. The South Ronaldsay Councillor, Cyril Annal, added that effectively they were saying everyone was innocent. The council's statement was seen as adding weight to the view that Paul Lee, would have to resign. Mr Lee had said in a statement on Wednesday 28th, that he would continue to work in the Department.

In a surprise announcement the day after the publication of the Report, the Royal Scottish Society for Prevention of Cruelty to Children said they were withdrawing from all investigations involving child abuse. They were, said their Chief Executive, Arthur Wood, moving away from this area of work because of the increasingly active role of the local authorities in child care cases. Liz McLean, who was responsible for much of the interviewing of the children, and who was severely criticised in the Report, took voluntary redundancy from the Society. Together with another ex-social worker she has set up a private consultancy for abused children in Edinburgh. Should another area for investigation not be the licensing of such agencies?

The Chief Constable of the Northern Constabulary, Hugh MacMillan, defended his officers' actions. They had, he said, been acting according to the Scottish Office guidelines, but in his opinion, they did not meet the particular circumstances in Orkney. He was unable to say more because of the threat of legal action against his force.

The four families had announced immediately after the Report was published that they would be claiming damages for the pain and suffering they had been caused. It was not immediately announced which bodies they would be taking action against at the Court of Session. They welcomed the criticisms in the Report, feeling themselves vindicated by Lord Clyde's findings. Their ongoing appeal to the European Commission on Human Rights passed another hurdle on its progress through the administrative red tape towards a ruling, and one of the fathers announced that he had applied to join Orkney Children's Panel.

All the families were trying to re-build their lives, and the adults and children were continuing to receive counselling from Dr John Powell of the Crichton Royal Hospital in Dumfries, who had worked extensively with those affected by the Lockerbie disaster. The parents called for an unreserved apology from the Social Work Department before better relationships could be established between the community and Orkney Islands Council. They said the whole island of South Ronaldsay had been slurred by Paul Lee, Gordon Sloan and the social workers, and that nothing less than a full apology would suffice.

Reverend Morris McKenzie, deeply disappointed with the Report, said he had been denied justice, and would like an investigation into why the Inquiry's remit had been so tightly drawn. He was also considering the possibility of legal action for damages, as well as appealing to the European Court to clear his name. He called for the social workers involved in the case to be sacked, saying no bridge-building was possible until this was done and repeated his anger at having to sit silently throughout the Inquiry. He felt the way he conducted his ministry had been deeply affected, and said he would never again willingly co-operate with the police.

On the floor of the House of Commons, Orkney's MP Jim Wallace welcomed the Report and its detail, but voiced his concern that suspicions still lingered, and said steps must be taken to allow these to be cleared.

The Social Work Team Leader Sue Millar resigned from Orkney Island Council and left the Department before the Inquiry began.

The Children's Hearing System in Orkney has a new Reporter. Hazel Marr was Deputy to Katherine Kemp when Gordon Sloan was appointed as Acting Reporter. Why, if she is now Reporter in her own right, was she not considered for the interim role? Mrs Kemp finally resigned after bizarre incidents concerning the disappearance of files and property, and considerable harassment. Gordon Sloan remains a Reporter with Strathclyde Region.

The press and media, while being the subject of much hostility from the agencies involved in the case, were not criticised by Lord Clyde in his Report. The remit demanded that he examine the effects of the publicity on those involved, but not the role of the journalists. It is arguable whether the Inquiry would ever have happened without the

attentions of the fourth estate, and at least one journalist said publicly
that she had hoped for more guidance on their role from Lord Clyde.

Meanwhile seven of the eight W children remained in care, and their
future was undecided. One of the boys appealed on his own behalf and
secured the discharge of his supervision order. He returned home to
Orkney. In view of all the criticism directed at Orkney Social Work
Department, the police and the RSSPCC, particularly with regard to the
interviewing techniques practised by the latter, and the policy of isolation
of siblings, the time had surely come for an urgent investigation into the
handling of the W family case.

Twenty-one months after the children were taken from their homes in
South Ronaldsay on 27 February 1991, there are still major concerns.
From the beginning people involved in child protection have repeated 'if
you knew what we know . . .' with the implication that what they knew
would condemn the families utterly. This cannot justify the actions taken
during the detention of the children. That phrase is part of a 'nod-nod,
wink-wink' syndrome and has no place in the vocabulary of anyone who
is involved in the care and protection of children. Another cop-out is the
bleating 'damned if we do, damned if we don't' cry of social workers.
If social workers do their jobs honestly, genuinely putting children's
interests above all else, then they will get it right. Honest mistakes can
be understood, kneejerk reactions to situations cannot. From the moment
the Inquiry in Orkney opened, the best interests of the children were
ignored by the agencies concerned in their panic to justify their actions.

After the Inquiry and Lord Clyde's Report, the Children's Hearing
System has an even more important role to play in child care and
protection. It is widely acknowledged that Social Work Departments
are under extreme pressure; pressure of workload, reorganisation, lack
of foster and community carers and ever-tightening budgets. In a climate
where decisions sometimes seem to be taken for the sake of expediency
because of these pressures, the Children's Panel remains the one body
which is capable of disregarding them and acting in the best interests of
the children. There is no doubt that the Children's Hearing System is
inadequately funded, and provides care and protection for children on
the cheap. This simply has to improve.

Twenty years old when the South Ronaldsay children were removed,
changes to the Hearing System to meet changing needs, may be necessary. The System has developed in different ways in different parts of
Scotland, probably because of the success of its confidentiality. This is
unacceptable, and any changes must strengthen the System and take it
towards 2000 in a unified manner. That will really be in the best interests
of the children.